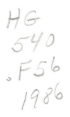

The Financial Analyst's Guide to Monetary Policy

The Financial Analyst's Guide to Monetary Policy

Edited by

Victor A. Canto
Charles W. Kadlec
and
Arthur B. Laffer

PRAEGER

PRAEGER SPECIAL STUDIES • PRAEGER SCIENTIFIC

New York • Westport, Connecticut • London

Library of Congress Cataloging-in-Publication Data
Main entry under title:

The Financial analyst's guide to monetary policy.

  Includes index.
  1. Monetary policy—United States—Addresses, essays,
lectures.   2. Supply-side economics—United States—
Addresses, essays, lectures.   I. Canto, Victor A.
II. Kadlec, Charles W.   III. Laffer, Arthur B.
HG540.F56   1986   332.4'973   85-28315
ISBN 0-275-92023-2

Library of Congress Catalog Card Number: 85-28315
ISBN: 0-275-92023-2

First published in 1986

Praeger Publishers, 521 Fifth Avenue, New York, NY 10175
A division of Greenwood Press, Inc.

Printed in the United States of America

∞™

The paper used in this book complies with the Permanent
Paper Standard issued by the National Information Standards
Organization (Z39.48-1984).

10 9 8 7 6 5 4 3 2 1

TO OUR CHILDREN

VERONICA MARIA CANTO
VICTORIA DE LOS ANGELES CANTO
VIANCA ANTONIA CANTO

BENJAMIN JOHN KADLEC
JASON CHARLES KADLEC

ALLISON BLAIR LAFFER
ARTHUR BETZ LAFFER
JUSTIN CHARLES LAFFER
MOLLY BETZ LAFFER
RACHEL VIRGINIA LAFFER
TRICIA MARGARET LAFFER

Preface

Most economics books that focus on the policy implications of government actions analyze those implications in the context of whether they offer the appropriate solution to the problem in question. Very seldom is policy analysis carried to the point where practical implications for business persons and financial analysts are clearly and fully derived.

In schools of business where economic courses are taught, this is an important issue. In general, students are unaware of how the knowledge of economics is translated into potential earnings.

A book such as this can, in some measure, fill that void. Our approach is straightfoward. In each chapter, we identify a particular policy problem and present an economic analysis of it. The second step—the one most economic books fail to take—is to draw the reader beyond the usual type of analysis and into a consideration of the practical implications and strategies that are vital to business managers, financial analysts, and investors in general.

In the process, the book provides a lucid presentation of incentive economics. We attempt to illustrate how incentives and disincentives affect economic behavior and the performance of the economy. In addition, we present a top–down approach that shows the reader how to trace the impact of government policies through the economy and thereby derive investment implications that will be helpful for investors and policymakers alike, from portfolio managers and financial analysts to corporate strategists and government officials.

This book focuses on monetary issues, and in particular on the real costs imposed on the economy by the Federal Reserve as it distorts the credit markets and reduces the flexibility of the financial system. The preferred policy would be for the Fed to target stabilization of the price level through an explicit, institutionalized price rule. The Fed should also provide for more efficient functioning of the credit markets through the elimination of restrictions that impair the functioning of the banking system, such as the imposition of non-interest-bearing reserve requirements, interest rate ceilings, and the like.

Above all, this book provides a succinct exposition of the monetary component of what has been known as supply-side economics. It provides a different perspective on the problems faced by the U.S. economy, as well as the solutions to the great economic problems of our time—inflation,

unemployment, and the instability of the financial markets. In addition
to presenting a guide to the better understanding of the effects of monetary policy on the overall economy, we have attempted to provide in these
chapters a policy prescription for sustained growth in the U.S. economy,
with no secular inflation and low interest rates, for the remainder of this
decade and into the next.

Victor A. Canto
Charles W. Kadlec
Arthur B. Laffer
Palos Verdes, California
June 30, 1985

Acknowledgments

This book is an outgrowth of ongoing research at A. B. Laffer Associates and the University of Southern California into the interactions between monetary policy and the financial markets. Over the years, we have benefited from the comments, suggestions, and contributions of many individuals and colleagues. We wish to thank our past and present colleagues at A. B. Laffer Associates, including Gerald Bollman, Thomas J. Gillespie, Kevin Melich, Thomas Nugent, and Wayne Steele Sharp, and our colleagues at the University of Southern California, who unselfishly read the manuscripts and contributed to the final product through their many comments and suggestions. We thank Edward P. Mooney for his tremendous help in editing and assembling the final manuscript, Margaret Hansen for her editorial assistance, and Sin Poe Soh for his statistical support. We also thank Dorothy Cooper and Lauren Welsh who aided in the production of the various stages of the manuscript.

Finally, we are grateful to the clients of A. B. Laffer Associates, without whose support this book would not have been possible.

Contents

List of Tables, Figures, and Graphs

TABLES

FIGURES

GRAPHS

1

The Monetary Crisis:
A Classical Perspective
Charles W. Kadlec and
Arthur B. Laffer

SUMMARY

A new kind of monetary crisis is enveloping the world's financial markets. Unlike the dollar monetary crises of the early 1970s, which marked the collapse of the fixed exchange rate system based on a dollar convertible into gold, all currencies now are suspect. The surge in the price of gold, inflation, and interest rates suggests the middle ground of floating exchange rates has been lost. What is left is a stark choice between anarchy in financial markets and a return to a dollar convertible into a monetary standard such as gold. To make the economy as "sound as a dollar," the dollar has to be made as "good as gold."

The new policies introduced by Federal Reserve Chairman Paul Volcker to defend the dollar offer little reason for optimism. By and large, they represent an increase in the effective tax rate on the activity levels of Federal Reserve member banks. The accompanying admonishments to the nation's bankers to restrain their lending activities and to limit increases in interest rates are a form of voluntary credit allocations that further undermine the utility of the dollar as an intermediary currency. Thus, the impulse for slower growth rates in the dollar monetary aggregates comes from diminished demand for dollars—a source that is per se inflationary. The omission of the demand for money from the analysis of inflation is as serious as the omission of the supply-side from the analysis of output.

What are required are policies that lead to an excess demand for dollars relative to their supply. Paying interest on member bank deposits at the Fed, ensuring the appreciation of the dollar relative to other currencies, and announcement of a return of dollar convertibility into gold at some specified future date would accomplish this objective. Inflationary expectations would fall precipitously, interest rates and the price of gold would drop, and equity values would surge. The potential gains are enormous: In 1965, for example, the yield on Corporate Aaa bonds was 4.5 percent, and the Dow Jones industrial average—in October 1979 dollars—was nearly 2,300. Failure to reverse the economic policies of the last 15 years, however, threatens further deterioration in the financial markets and in the economic outlook.

THE MONETARY CRISIS

The events of the last several years have served to make interest rates, reserve requirements, money supply targets, the value of the dollar on foreign exchange markets, and the price of gold topics of vital interest to financial analysts and corporate executives. This sudden fascination with the arcane nomenclature of monetary policy reflects continued dissatisfaction with the current monetary arrangements, and is symptomatic of a government policy in the midst of fundamental change.

The monetary experience since 1968, when the United States first allowed the market price of gold to diverge from its official price, can be thought of as a search for a system superior to the Bretton Woods fixed exchange rate system that prevailed from 1946 to its formal end in 1971. The two key elements of this system were that foreign central banks fixed their currency values to the dollar, thereby defining each currency's value. For its part, the United States was obligated to fix the dollar in terms of its exchange rate with gold—one dollar per one thirty-fifth ounce of gold. Thus, the value of each currency—both on the spot market and, in most cases, into the future—was known.

The first element to fall was the obligation of the United States to guarantee the value of the dollar in terms of gold. By 1973 all attempts to maintain fixed exchange rates collapsed.

Double-digit inflation and recession followed. Interest rates declined in 1976, but then began their climb toward new highs. A brief respite was gained in 1978, when the Carter administration, faced with an international crisis, patched together a program to defend the dollar on foreign exchange markets. For all of the U.S. promises to defend the dollar, however, that program served only to force foreign governments into pegging their revenues to a dollar that continued to fall in value.

Finally, in 1979 the monetary authorities abandoned their commitment to stabilizing interest rates in favor of targeting the quantity of money. The ensuing turmoil in the financial markets anticipated correctly a further deterioration in the U.S. economy and financial markets.

To understand the direction of policy, it frequently is useful to understand where policy has been. It can be assumed that the policymakers are in pursuit of success. Therefore, they can be expected to deemphasize policies that produce untoward effects while emphasizing those actions that bring about favorable results.

In that sense, the 1979 decision by Federal Reserve Chairman Paul Volcker to elevate targeting the monetary aggregates as the primary goal of monetary policy was the point most distant from the Bretton Woods monetary system. As such, it provides a useful departure point for an inquiry into the forces that are behind the ascendency of the new paradigm in monetary policy.

In October 1979 the Federal Reserve announced a policy to fight inflation by slowing the growth rate of the money supply:

- Reserve requirements on large-denomination time deposits were increased to 8 from 2 percent and extended to increases in member bank borrowings of Eurodollars, raising reserve requirements on these deposits to 8 from 0 percent.
- The discount rate was increased one full percentage point to 12 percent.
- The quantity of money measured by member bank reserves was the monetary variable elevated to center stage as the policy target.

In short, the Volcker initiatives of October 1979 were focused on domestic policy variables exclusively, in reaction to continued international pressures on the dollar. In addition to seeking to reduce the growth rate in bank reserves directly, the monetary authorities also began to ask for restraints in the creation of credit, anticipating the imposition of credit controls in March 1980. On the Monday afternoon and the Tuesday following the Volcker policy initiatives, the initial calm in the money markets and the fall in the price of gold were reversed as first Treasury Secretary G. William Miller and then Volcker admonished bankers to refrain from making loans to support "speculative activities" or "purely financial transactions" such as financing purchases of commodities or acquisitions of companies.

Fast money growth was responsible for rising inflation, it was argued. Therefore, by reducing the growth rate in money, inflation would be lowered. While interest rates might become somewhat more volatile, as soon as it became clear the Federal Reserve had the resolve to slow the growth in money, inflationary expectations and hence interest rates would decline as well.

The new policies introduced by Federal Reserve Chairman Volcker to defend the dollar, however, offered little reason for optimism. By and large, they represented an increase in the effective tax rate on the activity levels of Federal Reserve member banks. The accompanying admonishments to the nation's bankers to restrain their lending activities and to limit increases in interest rates were a form of voluntary credit allocations that further undermined the utility of the dollar as an intermediary currency. Thus, the impulse for slower growth rates in the dollar monetary aggregates comes from diminished demand for dollars—a source that is per se inflationary. The omission of the demand for money from the analysis of inflation is as serious as the omission of the supply side from the analysis of output. The financial markets were quick to sense this fatal flaw in the Fed's strategy (Table 1.1). During the weeks following the Volcker announcement, the Dow Jones industrial average fell 58.6 points, or 6.5 percent. Precipitous declines in the stock market are more often than not accompanied by periods of equally as precipitous declines in real economic profits and followed by periods of economic contraction (Laffer and Ranson 1977).

Interest rate movements also signaled increased uncertainty and heightened fears of inflation. In the month following the change in policy, short-term rates rose by nearly 1.5 percentage points to 12.44 percent, while long-term rates jumped a then-unheard-of 1 percentage point to 10.33 percent.

The price of gold was slower to respond, first rising by $10 to $395 per ounce but then declining back below $390 per ounce. Within four months, however, an ounce of gold would sell for a record $850 in Europe and $875 in New York.

TABLE 1.1. The Markets' Response to the Volcker Initiative

	October 5	October 12	November 9
Dow Jones Industrials	897.6	839.0	806.5
3-Month Treasury Bills (Yield)	10.96%	11.72%	12.44%
30-Year Treasury Notes (Yield)	9.35%	9.74%	10.33%
Price of Gold (London P.M. Fixing)	$385.00	$395.00	$389.50
Cents per German Mark	56.89¢	55.76¢	55.73¢

Source: Wall Street Journal.

The dollar's exchange rate did stabilize. But that stability could be attributed to the commitment of foreign central banks to cooperate in the stabilization of the dollar's value. Indeed, in the aftermath of the Volcker initiative, interest rates rose throughout the industrialized world, suggesting that inflation would be worse, not better, globally.

The financial market's anticipation of slower economic growth and higher inflation proved all too true. Economic growth slowed abruptly in the last quarter of 1979, and then contracted at a 9.6 percent annual rate with the imposition of credit controls during the second quarter of 1980.

The monthly average rate for three-month Treasury bills finally peaked in May 1981 at 16.3 percent, while 20-year government bond yields posted their highest monthly average of 15.3 percent in October 1981.

Finally, far from slowing, the rate of inflation soared. In January 1980 the annual rate of advance in the consumer and producer price indexes hit new highs of 18 and 21 percent, respectively.

THE "MONEYNESS" OF MONEY

Money performs at least two essential functions: It serves both as a medium of exchange and as a store of value. As a medium of exchange, money is that one commodity from which movement into any other commodity is accomplished at the least possible cost. Therefore, money facilitates market transactions at the lowest possible cost when used in market exchanges. Money's function is to mesh income and expenditure streams.

The more efficient a money is in performing these two functions, the greater its "moneyness." An increase in a currency's moneyness will make it more useful, thereby increasing the demand for it; the more readily acceptable it is or the more stable its purchasing power, the money will lead to a reduction in the demand for the money balances held in that numeraire. A fall in the velocity of money (output divided by the quantity of money) is symptomatic of an increase in a currency's moneyness and vice versa.

In today's integrated financial markets, the demand for a currency is truly global in nature. Corporations, international businesses, some individuals, and even government agencies can choose the currency they wish to hold. From one day to the next, billions of dollars in money balances can flow from one currency to another as corporations, central banks, and other transactors change their preferences as to the currency in which they do business or the currency in which to store their liquid balances. Thus, the day-to-day flux in the global demand for a currency—including the dollar—can be far greater than the change in the actual amount of that currency supplied by monetary authorities. It is in this context that the actions of the U.S. monetary authorities and the reactions of the financial markets should be viewed.

The Fed's Actions in a Conceptual Context

The major thrust of the Fed's actions in November 1979 was to constrain the growth in the money supply by raising the effective cost of financial intermediation to member banks. By raising the discount rate, it explicitly raised the cost to member banks when they borrowed non-interest-bearing assets. Furthermore, the Fed, by increasing reserve requirements, increased the share of total member bank assets that must be held in non-interest-bearing form. The Fed, in effect, raised tax rates on the activity levels of its member banks.

The one-percentage point increase in the discount rate to a record 12 percent is not an especially significant part of the Fed's moves, even though it was described widely as the most important part of both the November 1978 and October 1979 policy initiatives. Borrowings at the Fed by member banks account for only a small fraction of total bank liabilities. These borrowings average less than 5 percent of outstanding certificates of deposit, a major source of funds for banks.

Moreover, the Fed has never been willing to lend unlimited amounts to member banks, even if those banks were willing to pay the discount rate. The Fed allocates the reserves it is willing to lend to its member banks according to other criteria. Basically, the discount rate is only one part of the total cost faced by member banks when borrowing reserves. It still is a cost, however, and should be analyzed as such.

The eight-percentage point increase in reserve requirements to 16 percent on increases in certain large domestic deposits and to 8 percent on increases in Eurodollar deposits is more important. Even if imposed only on incremental deposits, it has a pervasive impact. On the asset side of member banks' portfolios, a large portion of assets must now be held on deposit in the Federal Reserve. The critical feature of these deposits is that they are non-interest bearing. The greater the reserve requirements are, the smaller the portion of bank assets that earn income. An increase in reserve requirements is simply an increase in the tax rate on the activities of member banks.

The actual tax rate effects are quite consequential. They depend on both the reserve requirement ratio and the level of interest rates. For required reserves, the equivalent effective marginal tax on the gross earnings of banks is equal to the share of the bank's total assets held in reserve times the bank's average lending rate. For borrowed reserves, there is an additional effective tax rate that corresponds to the discount rate times the share borrowed reserves are of the bank's total liabilities.

When stated thusly, the consequences of the Fed's actions should be readily apparent. To visualize the effects the Fed's actions would have on the overall money markets, imagine what would happen if tax rates on increases in member bank activity levels were to be progressively escalated until they reached 100 percent. Quite obviously, once the tax reached 100 percent, there would no longer be any increase in the activity levels of the banks. They would cease to expand. As the tax rates went even higher, member banks would be forced to charge their customers ever greater amounts per additional dollar borrowed. Yet, the banks' incremental business would become progressively less profitable.

As implied by basic tax theory, the higher the rate of taxation on the production of any product, the greater will be the price paid by the demanders of that product and the lower will be the price received by the suppliers of that product. Taxes introduce a wedge between prices paid and prices received.

Quantity responses to the Fed's actions will occur in lockstep with these price responses. The higher the price demanders must pay, the less they will demand. Symmetrically, the lower the price suppliers receive, the less they will supply. Thus, the Fed's actions will reduce unambiguously the supply of and also the demand for member bank assets (such as loans) and member bank liabilities (such as demand deposits), reducing the activity level of member banks.

In other words, the effect of the Volcker initiative was to impair the ability of member banks to perform their central economic function: providing intermediary services between lenders and borrowers of dollars. As a result, both lenders and borrowers were expected to seek other, now more efficient financial intermediation.

What this meant is that lending and borrowing shifted out of member banks toward nonmember banks, and from dollars into foreign currencies such as the mark, yen, and Swiss franc. The lower the profit rate from producing member bank assets, the more banks will shift their activities to higher-profit substitutes. Subsequently member banks attempted to leave the Federal Reserve System. Banks that were not member banks and therefore were not subject to the Fed's reserve requirements expanded more rapidly than those banks that were members.

The availability of substitutes for member bank liabilities and assets outside of the United States extended this shift even further. Both demanders and suppliers of credit could substitute out of dollars held in member banks into Eurodollar accounts, foreign currency-denominated balances, indexed accounts, and gold. In short, the Fed's actions reduced the viability and attractiveness of the dollar, and especially of dollars produced by member banks. As such, the Fed's actions per se have increased the prospects for inflation, in spite of the fact that their actions resulted in a slower growth in the measured quantity of money. During the two quarters prior to the Volcker initiative, M1 grew at a seasonally adjusted annual rate of 11.2 and 9.4 percent, respectively. By contrast, the two quarters after the initiative, M1 grew at a seasonally adjusted annual rate of 3.1 and 6.3 percent, respectively.

There are numerous ways in which the rate of growth of the quantity of money can be reduced. Some of those ways will reduce the prospects for future inflation. Some methods of reducing the growth rate of money supply will have a minimal effect on the rate of inflation. There are, however, also ways of reducing the rate of growth of the measured money supply that are inflationary. The Fed chose a method of reducing money growth rates that was inflationary.

Consider for a moment the market for liabilities of member banks of the Federal Reserve System. As illustrated in Figure 1.1, the demand for these liabilities depends in part on the yield the holders of these liabilities receive. Therefore, the supply of deposits banks receive is upward sloping and depends upon the total payment (services inclusive) per dollar deposited paid by the banks to their depositors. The banks' demand for these deposits depends upon the net interest income banks can anticipate per dollar of assets deployed. Thus, the banks' demand for deposits depends in part upon the price they must pay for the funds, including the cost of holding a portion of those deposits in non-interest-bearing reserve accounts. The supply of deposits, on the other hand, depends solely on the yield depositors receive before the calculation of this de facto tax.

In Figure 1.1, the initial equilibrium position is illustrated. Here the demand for and supply of money are in balance at the quantity of money M and at the price of money P. Instead of interest rates, the price of money as represented by P is the inverse of the price level measured by, say, the consumer price index or the producer price index; that is, it is

FIGURE 1.1. **Money Market Equilibrium**

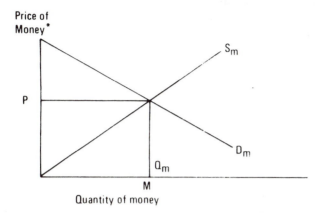

*The purchasing power of money (inverse of the price level).
Source: Author's calculations

the purchasing power of money. Thus, a rise in the price of money is equivalent to a decline in the overall price level. Symmetrically, when the price of money falls, this corresponds to an increase in the general price level for the economy as a whole, or inflation.

The monetarists' perception of a reduction in the overall money supply is depicted in Figure 1.2. In this instance, money supply is shifted back from S to S^1 while money demand remains unchanged. The consequences of such an action are an increase in the price of money from P to P^1 (that is, a fall in the economy's price level) and a concomitant reduction in the equilibrium quantity of money from M to M^1.

In Figure 1.3, money demand shifts back (from D to D^1) along with the backward shift in money supply. There will be no change in the price level in spite of the reduction in the quantity of money.

In Figure 1.4, however, only money demand shifts back. In this situation, the fall in the quantity of money occurs as the price of money falls from P to P^3, or, if you will, as the overall price level in the economy rises.

The basic point is straightforward enough: If there is a decrease in the quantity of any good supplied, its price should rise as the equilibrium quantity of that good falls. If, however, there is a decrease in the demand for any good, less will be forthcoming as its price falls. Given the change in the quantity of the product, the change in the product's price depends upon the origins of the disturbance. If the disturbance originates in the demand for the product, quantity and price will be positively related. If

FIGURE 1.2. Effects of a Money Supply Shift on the Money Market Equilibrium

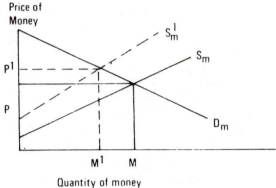

Quantity of money

Source: Author's calculations

the disturbance originates in the supply of the product, quantity and price will be inversely related. On a conceptual level, Fed policies that result in a slower growth rate of the money supply are as likely to lead to higher as to lower inflation.

The Volcker initiatives of early October 1979 almost certainly were inflationary. The policy changes were quite able to slow the growth in the quantity of dollars. But the Fed's policies achieved this result largely by decreasing the demand for dollars. By raising tax rates on U.S.-produced dollars, the Fed caused a substitution into alternative forms of

FIGURE 1.3. Effects of Demand and Supply Shifts on the Money Market Equilibrium

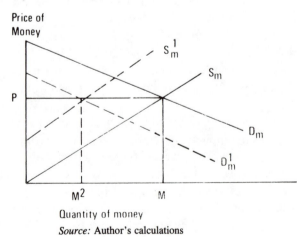

Quantity of money

Source: Author's calculations

**FIGURE 1.4. Effects of a Demand Shift
on the Money Market Equilibrium**

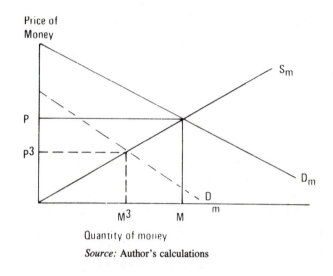

Source: Author's calculations

money to back transactions. This substitution out of dollars meant that there would be fewer dollars and each dollar would be worth less; that is, the price level would rise (Laffer 1977). Inflation increased because the reduction in the growth of money resulted from a diminution in the demand for dollars relative to their supply.

What Constitutes an Appropriate Monetary Policy?

From the standpoint of the entire U.S. economy, the appropriate policy for bringing inflation under control is one that increases the demand for money relative to its supply ex ante. The creation of an incipient excess demand for the liabilities of the Fed will, of necessity, lead to a rise in the price of money and therefore a fall in the rate of inflation. What happens to the quantity of money under such circumstances depends upon the state of the economy.

If the economy is producing at its fullest potential, investment rates are high and unemployment rates low; and if the real value of capital assets is at their ceiling levels all during a period when there are no close substitutes for money in existence, then an appropriate monetary policy designed to bring inflation to task may well correspond to less money in the economy.

An appropriate monetary policy designed to stop inflation, however, could just as readily result in a substantial increase in the overall quantity of money. If the policy is appropriate, it will encourage a dramatic rise in output as well as a dramatic increase in the demand for dollars per unit of domestic output as money holders worldwide move back into the dollar. The velocity of money in the United States would decline. The fall in the rate of inflation would result primarily from increased demand for money and therefore would concurrently lead to an increase in the total quantity of money.

At current prices, if the dollar were literally assured of being as good as gold, nearly everyone would hold dollars and not gold. Likewise, if interest rates were low, reflecting the lowering of inflationary anticipations, far wider use of dollar money balances would occur. The use of foreign currencies to support international transactions or simply as a store of value also would diminish as the dollar was restored to its position as the international numeraire. A successful monetary policy would shift the demand for money and necessitate an increase in the dollar money supply. Inflation would be brought quickly under control.

The market indicators of an appropriately designed monetary policy would be a fall in interest rates, including an especially large fall in the longer-term end of the spectrum. The stock market should post major gains. The dollar price of gold would fall, and, if anything, the dollar would advance robustly on foreign exchange markets.

The Path to Stable Prices

The experiences during this decade of Germany, Switzerland, and Japan provide the outline of a successful monetary policy. After the gold window was shut by the United States in August 1971, the major countries of the world negotiated a new set of fixed parities. These were formalized in the Smithsonian agreement of December 1971. It was similar to the Bretton Woods system in that foreign central banks remained responsible for maintaining the parity of their currency with the dollar. What was different from Bretton Woods was that the United States had no responsibility for maintaining the value of the dollar in terms of gold or any other monetary standard. In addition, the price bands around which currencies were permitted to fluctuate were widened.

The commitment to maintain parity with the dollar resulted in German, Swiss, Japanese, and other central banks buying billions of dollars and increasing their money supplies. During 1972 foreign exchange reserves of the industrial countries jumped by 15 percent. The rate of inflation increased throughout the world.

In an attempt to slow the inflow of dollars and curb inflation, Germany, Switzerland, and Japan imposed foreign exchange controls and various forms of credit allocations and sharply increased reserve requirements on their domestic banks' liabilities. Then, in early 1973 the Smithsonian agreement collapsed as first Switzerland, Italy, and then Germany, Japan, and other countries allowed their currencies to float against the dollar.

For the first time in more than two decades, the monetary authorities of the industrialized world were without the monetary standard of fixing the value of their currency to the dollar. During 1973 Germany, Switzerland, and Japan adopted monetary policies similar to the Fed's most recent initiative: the elevation of controlling the quantity of money to a key policy variable. The hoped-for result was to cut their currencies from the dollar and the inflationary monetary policies of the Fed.

These countries also attempted to limit the appreciation of their currencies by continuing, and in some cases increasing, credit controls, especially on international exchange. In January 1973, for example, Germany imposed limits on foreign purchases of German securities, including stocks, from Germans; direct investment in Germany by foreign corporations; and the use of the mark by Germans as the numeraire for credit, including payment terms, involving nonresident creditors. The "moneyness" of these currencies was diminished, and demand for them fell. The growth in money supplies slowed dramatically, but wholesale price inflation ballooned as velocity, the ratio of national income to money balances, rose (Graph 1.1).

Beginning in 1974—under pressure of contracting economies—many of these policies were reversed. Reserve requirements in Germany, Switzerland, and Japan were reduced, foreign exchange controls were eased, and their currencies were allowed to appreciate. The rate of inflation in all three countries fell precipitously. This was expected. What was unexpected was the sudden decline in wholesale prices that ensued in early 1975 in Switzerland and Japan and the near decline in Germany. As a result, all three countries were forced in one way or another to abandon their commitment to a stable growth in the quantity of money, and adopt a monetary policy based on stabilizing the price level—to prevent deflation as well as inflation.

Nowhere was this change more striking than in Switzerland. There, money supply growth, which had jumped by 20 percent in 1971, was brought to less than 1 percent in 1973. But the rate of wholesale price inflation accelerated to more than 20 percent in the fourth quarter of 1973 from less than 10 percent per year in 1972. During this period, the Swiss imposed various kinds of credit controls including prohibiting Swiss banks

GRAPH 1.1. Changes in the Velocity of Money in Germany, Japan, and Switzerland

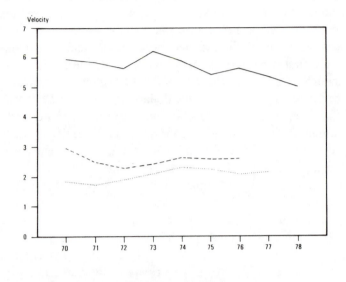

_____ German national income divided by money balances.
------ Japanese national income divided by money balances.
. . . . . . Swiss national income divided by money balances.

Source: International Financial Statistics, Bureau of Statistics, International Monetary Fund, Washington, D.C.

from lending newly acquired franc deposits (Northrup 1973). Beginning in 1974 these controls were dismantled. While money growth remained flat, inflation plummeted until, in the first quarter of 1975, wholesale prices declined at a near double-digit annual pace (Graph 1.2).

At this point, the Swiss were forced to abandon the quantity rule for monetary policy, arguing that the Swiss franc had become "overvalued." As a result, Swiss monetary authorities intervened, buying billions of dollars in foreign exchange markets and, in the process, expanding their monetary base and money supply. The effect of this change was to put Swiss monetary policy onto a de facto "price rule." When wholesale prices began to fall, the Swiss intervened, increasing their money supply. Conversely, when wholesale prices began to advance, intervention ceased and money supply growth slowed.

Between 1974 and the third quarter of 1978, the growth rate in the Swiss money supply went from relative stability to instability, vacillat-

GRAPH 1.2. Money and Inflation in Switzerland

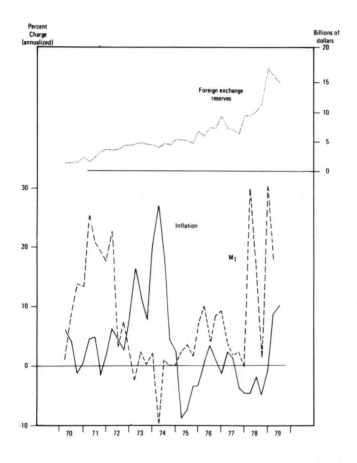

_____ Wholesale prices: quarterly change at annualized rates.
------ M1 seasonally adjusted: quarter to quarter change at annualized rates.
. . . . . . Foreign exchange reserves.

Source: International Financial Statistics, Bureau of Statistics, International Monetary Fund, Washington, D.C.: Federal Reserve Bank of St. Louis.

ing from near 0 percent during 1974 to 30 percent in the second quarter of 1978. At the same time, the rate of change in wholesale prices, which had been volatile, became relatively stable (Graph 1.2).

It is difficult to understand the relationship of changes in money supply and prices in Switzerland by analyzing the Swiss economy. But when they are placed in a global context, the lesson becomes clear. With the abandonment of the dollar standard in 1973, the commitment to maintain the purchasing power of the Swiss franc, and the relaxation of credit controls in 1974, the moneyness of the Swiss franc increased relative to the dollar. The result was the substitution into Swiss francs by holders of money balances throughout the world. Thus, when the Swiss intervened to suppress the rise in the value of the franc and stop the fall in wholesale prices, the monetary authorities were inadvertently accommodating global shifts in demand for Swiss francs, which had little, if anything, to do with the level of economic activity in Switzerland,

Not suprisingly, the price of gold in Swiss francs during this period (1975–78) also remained relatively stable, even as the dollar price of gold doubled. This indicates that a monetary policy based on stabilizing wholesale prices is a close substitute for the gold standard and vice versa.

EVENTS IN A BROAD HISTORICAL CONTEXT

The chaotic state of the financial markets in 1979 and 1980 dramatized the long-standing deterioration in the U.S. economy. In the mid-1960s, the stock market in constant dollars was two and one-half times higher than it was at the end of 1979. Inflation rates had increased by tenfold. The prime interest rate, which stood at 4.5 percent in 1965, peaked at 21.5 percent in December 1980. Other interest rates mirrored the pattern embodied in the prime (Graph 1.3).

Gold sold for $35 per ounce in 1965. In February 1980, it sold for nearly 25 times that figure. Exchange rates also tumbled, again at increasingly rapid rates. The startling feature of U.S. financial markets in 1979 and 1980 was not that something new was happening—it wasn't. The startling feature was that it was happening at an accelerated pace (Graph 1.4).

The dramatic decline of the U.S. economy is exactly what one would expect when an economy is subjected to increasingly heavy doses of the wrong medicine. Bad economic theory renders bad economic prescriptions. These misguided prescriptions had become dominant since the mid-1960s. The worse the performance turned in by the economy, the larger the dose of bad economic policies the politicians prescribed. The consequences were predictable.

The Kennedy administration in the early 1960s cut personal income tax rates by some 25 percent. It also maintained the dollar's convertibility into gold. The overall economy experienced prolonged rapid real

GRAPH 1.3. Inflation and the Prime Rate

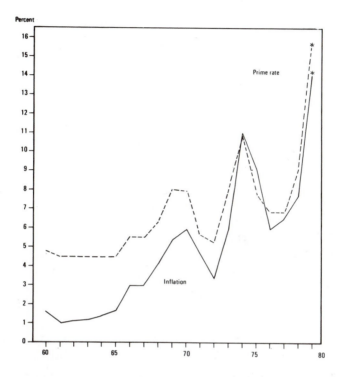

*Latest data available as of November 9, 1979.

———— Annual change in the consumer price index.
------ Average prime rate.

Sources: Survey of Current Business, United States Department of Commerce, Bureau of Economic Analysis, Government Printing Office, Washington, D.C.; *Economic Report of the President, 1979,* U.S. Government Printing Office, Washington, D.C.

growth with a very low rate of inflation (Graph 1.5). Government spending as a percentage of gross national product fell even as total spending in absolute dollars was growing rapidly.

Subsequently, effective tax rates were increased and new tax rates were imposed where they did not exist before. The average effective marginal tax rate (Federal, state, and local) on labor rose to 44.3 percent in 1978 from 33.5 percent in 1965 (Kadlec et al. 1978). At the same time, the worth of the dollar was undermined by deliberately severing its link to gold and by purposely devaluing it in the foreign exchange markets. The worse things got, the more the dollar was devalued, the higher tax

GRAPH 1.4. The Price of Gold and the Value of the Dollar

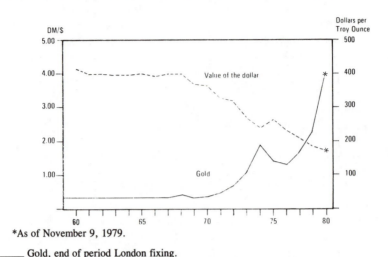

*As of November 9, 1979.

———— Gold, end of period London fixing.
------ German marks per dollar, end of year market rate.

Sources: International Financial Statistics, Bureau of Statistics, International Monetary Fund, Washington, D.C.; *Wall Street Journal.*

rates were raised, and the louder were the official denunciations of gold. The economic consequences surfaced quickly. Inflation rose, productivity declined, and the economy stagnated. The life signs of the economy flagged. The stock market, for one, sank while interest rates soared. In 1965 the Dow Jones industrials converted into 1979's devalued dollar was nearly 2,300, and Corporate Aaa bonds yielded just 4.5 percent. Gold, it was soon found, had not been propped up by the dollar, but, in fact, the reverse was true: Gold had propped up the value of the dollar (Graph 1.6).

APPENDIX
THE IMPORTANCE OF
THE INTERVENTION MECHANISM

Foreign exchange support operations can be extremely important in the implementation of a successful monetary policy initiative. The intervention mechanism is critical. Depending upon the specifics, foreign exchange intervention can result in a healthy form of discipline on countries with easy money problems, or it can lead to the pervasive spread of unsound policies. The critical considerations are, first, which coun-

GRAPH 1.5. Real Growth, Productivity, and Unemployment

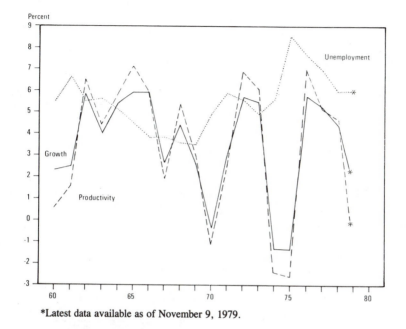

*Latest data available as of November 9, 1979.

—————— Annual growth in real gross national product.
— — — — Annual change in productivity of private business sector.
. . . . . . Average unemployment rate.

Source: Economic Report of the President, 1979, U.S. Government Printing Office, Washington, D.C.

try does the intervention and, second, what affect this intervention has on each respective country's monetary policies.

In the case of, say, a weak dollar and a strong German mark, there are two ways in which the dollar/mark exchange rate can be supported. Either the Bundesbank can do the intervention, or the Federal Reserve can be the intervening agent. If the Germans accept responsibility for stabilizing the exchange and carry out the intervention, their monetary policy will effectively be adapted to the monetary policy of the United States. If, on the other hand, the United States carries out the intervention—and does not offset it with open market operations—then it will be the U.S. monetary policy that adjusts to the German.

In the case where the Germans support a weak dollar, they purchase dollars (acquire U.S. private bank liabilities) in the foreign exchange mar-

GRAPH 1.6. Tax Rates, Government Spending, and the Stock Market

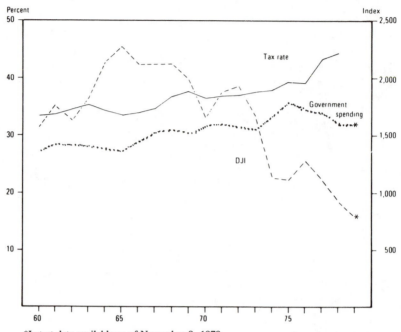

*Latest data available as of November 9, 1979.

_____ Weighted average marginal effective tax rate on labor (Federal, state and local).
. . . . . . Total government expenditures as a percentage of gross national product.
------ Dow Jones industrial average expressed in October 1979 dollars.

Sources: Economic Report of the President, 1979, U.S. Government Printing Office, Washington, D.C.; *The "Prototype Wedge Model"™: A Tool for Supply-Side Economics,* H. C. Wainwright & Co. Economics, Boston.

ket. They pay for these dollars by creating German marks (German private bank liabilities). The Bundesbank, however, does not retain possession of these private U.S. bank liabilities. The dollar deposits are used to acquire dollar-denominated interest-bearing securities, reintroducing the dollars they acquired in the foreign exchange market back into private circulation. The dollar money supply remains unchanged. The German mark money supply as a result increases. Thus, when the Bundesbank stabilizes the foreign exchange value of the dollar, it is forced to inflate the German mark to match the inflation of the dollar.

When the Federal Reserve does the intervention to support the dollar, the precise reverse occurs. In this instance, the Fed, acting as an agent for the Treasury Department, would issue German mark liabilities in the private capital market, obtaining mark deposits at private banks in exchange for its liabilities. The Fed would then buy U.S. dollars with its newly acquired mark deposits. The mark deposits would be returned summarily to private hands, thereby leaving the German mark money supply unaltered. The Fed now would own additional dollar deposits, thus removing them from private hands and reducing the U.S. monetary base and money supply. In total, then, if the United States does the intervention, the inflation of the dollar will, of necessity, be reduced to the inflation of the mark.

Any one of these economic results from the specific intervention schemes could be reversed by open market operations. If, for example, the Fed were to be the intervening agent to bolster a sagging dollar and yet simultaneously increased its open market purchases of bonds, the beneficial effects of the intervention would be offset and the dollar would continue to sag. In the same vein, if the Germans were to be the intervening agent while at the same time the Fed were, as a result, to sell bonds in the open market, the beneficial effects would reappear. In any event, the policies of both central banks must be analyzed in concert (Laffer and Ranson 1979).

REFERENCES

Babin, Charles E., and Arthur B. Laffer. 1979. "Inflation," *Economic Study,* H. C. Wainwright & Co. Economics, Boston (July).

"Germany Erects Barriers to U.S. Dollar As Greenback Is Buffeted in World Markets." 1973. *Wall Street Journal* (February 5): p.7.

Kadlec, Charles W., Arthur B. Laffer, and Marc A. Miles. 1978. "The Carter Turnaround: A New Policy for the Dollar," *Economic Study,* H. C. Wainwright & Co. Economics, Boston (December).

Laffer, Arthur B. 1977. "Substitution of Monies in Demand; The Case of Mexico," *Economic Study,* H. C. Wainwright & Co. Economics, Boston (May).

Laffer, Arthur B., and David R. Ranson. 1979. "The Prototype Wedge Model: A Tool for Supply-Side Economics," *Special Study,* H. C. Wainwright & Co. Economics, Boston (September).

———. 1977. "Some Practical Applications of the Efficient-Market Concept," *Economic Study,* H. C. Wainwright & Co. Economics, Boston (July).

Northrup, Bowen. 1973. "Swiss Float Franc, Markets Are Nervous," *Wall Street Journal* (January 24): p.40.

Wanniski, Jude. 1977. "The Volcker Panic," *The Political Economy in Perspective,* H. C. Wainwright & Co. Economics, Boston (May).

2
What Monetarism Has Done to Us
Paul Evans

SUMMARY

In October 1979, the Federal Reserve adopted a policy of targeting monetary aggregates. This ended a policy of stabilizing interest rates and led to three years of economic stagnation. This study quantifies the changes in economic activity brought about by this change in Federal Reserve policy.

The importance of both money growth and interest rate volatility is examined. The correlation between real gross national product (GNP) and money growth volatility is not found to be statistically significant. On the other hand, the correlation between real GNP and volatility in long-term interest rates is highly significant by statistical standards. The increase in interest rate volatility evident in the 1979–82 period, in all likelihood, contributed to the severity of the 1980–82 recession.

Money growth higher than the public has anticipated also is associated with an appreciable increase in output, and money growth less than anticipated is associated with lower output. In addition, increased interest rate volatility lowers output in future years.

A model based on these results forecasted that the economy would expand at a 5.7 percent rate in 1984 and by 4.4 percent in 1985. It suggested that the boom in 1984 would be due, in large part, to a reduction in interest rate volatility.

The obvious policy recommendation is that the Federal Reserve should make interest rate stability one of its policy goals. At the same time, the Fed must be able to respond intelligently to information available to it about other important economic variables, including sensitive commodity prices and the pace of economic growth.

WHAT MONETARISM HAS DONE TO US

On October 6, 1979, the Federal Reserve began a policy of targeting monetary aggregates and ended a policy of stabilizing interest rates. Then, for three years the U.S. economy stagnated. The results of this study strongly suggest that this stagnation occurred not so much because the Federal Reserve slowed money growth, thereby imposing disinflation on the economy. Rather, the stagnation appears to have resulted in large part from the sharp rise in interest rate volatility that occurred after the Federal Reserve stopped stabilizing interest rates. By contrast, no evidence is found to support the claim that increased volatility of money growth contributed to stagnation. A reasonable conclusion is therefore that the Federal Reserve should more strongly emphasize the stability of interest rates.

Stable Money Growth Versus Stable Interest Rates

The change in monetary policy toward targeting monetary aggregates was followed by increased volatility in money growth and interest rates. In general, monetarists criticized the Fed for fluctuations in money growth, arguing that this increased volatility raised the variability of economic activity, contributed to uncertainty, and undermined the credibility of central banks (Meltzer 1982; Friedman 1982a; Friedman 1982b). Increased volatility in money growth was not the only source of increased criticism. With the October 1979 policy change, interest rates also became markedly more volatile. Many nonmonetarists think that this increased interest rate volatility stemmed primarily from the change in operating procedures that accompanied the change in policy (Evans 1981).

Interest rate volatility, they argued, made bonds much riskier and hence raised the risk premia in interest rates (Friedman 1982). In addition, highly volatile interest rates made it more difficult for lenders and borrowers to agree upon the interest rates at which to transact with each other. This resulting disruption of the capital markets reduced their efficiency and breadth. Finally, businesses faced with interest rates that could change drastically in a short time found it much harder to plan production ahead. The combination of higher real interest rates, less efficient capital markets, and greater difficulty in planning production led to lower output, thereby depressing the economy unnecessarily.

Measures of Money Growth and Interest Rate Volatility

In order to assess these two positions, measures of money growth and interest rate volatility are first created. Then, the evolution of the volatility of each series over the postwar period is examined. Finally, statistical tests are performed to determine whether the volatility of either money or interest rates can explain changes in output growth.

The standard deviations of monthly growth in the M1 money supply and monthly changes in Moody's bond rate are used as the measures of volatility, calculated from the 12 monthly observations for each year.

For the 1947–82 period, the volatility of money growth fluctuated widely—between 0.0010 and 0.0088. For the entire 25 years, the standard deviation averaged 0.0028. It reached peaks in 1947, 1954, 1959, 1966, 1970, 1973, 1975, and 1980; it reached troughs in 1950, 1957, 1961, 1968, 1971, 1974, and 1977 (Graph 2.1). This pattern of peaks and troughs seems not to coincide with the business cycle in any close way. Indeed, money growth volatility fluctuates more frequently than economic activity. The years 1980, 1981, and 1982 stand out because money growth was much more volatile then than it had been previously. The change in monetary policy on October 6, 1979, preceded a sharp rise in money growth volatility.

Interest rate volatility followed a jagged, upward-sloping path from 1946, when the Federal Reserve was still supporting bond prices, to 1958, when it no longer was. This upward trend was reversed in the next six years. Indeed, interest rate volatility was as low between 1963 and 1965 as it has ever been in the postwar period (Graph 2.2). Perhaps coincidentally—but perhaps not—the Kennedy–Johnson administration was reducing tax rates at this time. Interest rate volatility then soared as the Vietnam War escalated, reaching a peak in 1969. During the next ten years, interest rate volatility averaged 0.10, a value comparable with its peak value in the 1950s. It oscillated about that average with considerable amplitude, however. Finally, following the change in monetary policy on October 6, 1979, interest rate volatility surged. In 1980, 1981, and 1982, it averaged 0.58, more than seven times larger than its average between 1947 and 1978.

It is difficult to draw any strong conclusions from these data alone. Interest rate volatility does appear to be a better candidate as a determinant

GRAPH 2.1. Volatility of Money Growth

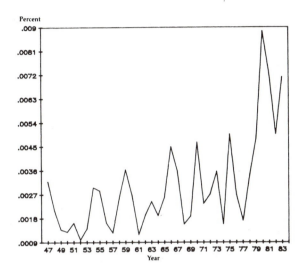

_____ Standard deviation of month-to-month M1 growth.

Source: Author's calculations

of output than is money growth volatility. Over the postwar period, interest rate volatility has tended to be low when the economy was performing well (before 1958 and in the mid-1960s) and has tended to be high when the economy was performing poorly (in the late 1950s, after 1969, and especially after 1979). In contrast, money growth volatility has a cycle length appreciably shorter than that of economic activity.

Volatility and Output

The analysis testing the relative importance of money growth and interest rate volatility begins with an adaption of the standard monetarist model of the economy as developed by Barro (1978) and modified by the author.[1] The output equation of this model (Table 2.1; Equation 1) relates the log of real GNP to t, a time trend; ln $Y(-1)$, the log of the previous year's real GNP; UMG, a measure of unanticipated money growth for the current year; $UMG(-1)$, unanticipated money growth for the previous year; and ln G, the log of real Federal government purchases of goods

GRAPH 2.2. Volatility of Interest Rates

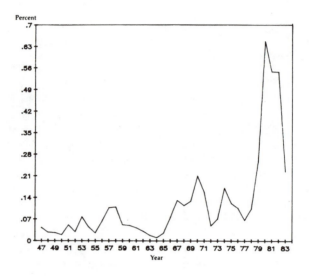

_____ Standard deviation of month-to-month changes in Moody's bond rates.

Source: Author's calculations

and services. Each of these variables is statistically significant. Unanticipated money growth in both the current and the previous years affects output, as do Federal purchases. The inclusion of the previous year's real GNP indicates that output undergoes persistent movements that stem not only from unanticipated money growth and federal purchases, but also from other causes.

The significance of the volatility of money growth and the volatility of interest rates is tested by adding each variable to this basic equation. A *t* statistic (in parentheses) larger than 2 in magnitude indicates statistical significance. The results include the following:

- The regression coefficients for the current and the previous year's money growth volatilities [*MGV* and *MGV*(-1)] are not statistically or economically significant (Table 2.1, Equations 2 to 4). Monetarists are probably wrong in believing that money growth volatility depresses economic activity.

TABLE 2.1. Testing for the Importance of Volatility in Money Growth and Interest Rates for Output

$\ln Y = 3.10 + 0.0183T + 0.439\ln Y(-1) + 1.11UMG + 1.02UMG(-1) + .0371\ln G$ (1)
   (4.55)(4.43)   (3.62)   (3.99)   (3.60)   (2.28)

$R^2 = 0.998$, SE $= 0.0194$, DW $= 1.61$

$\ln Y = 3.05 + 0.0182T + 0.446\ln Y(-1) + 1.06UMG + 1.02UMG(-1) + 0.0350\ln G \quad -0.00403\ln MGV$ (2)
   (4.35)(4.35)   (3.60)   (3.60)   (3.52)   (2.05)   (-0.47)

$R^2 = 0.998$, SE $= 0.0197$, DW $= 1.67$

$\ln Y = 3.09 + 0.0182T + 0.441\ln Y(-1) + 1.10UMG + 1.01UMG(-1) + .0363\ln G \quad -0.00098\ln MGV(-1)$ (3)
   (4.42)(4.35)   (3.54)   (3.91)   (3.33)   (2.03)   (-0.12)

$R^2 = 0.998$, SE $= .0198$, DW $= 1.63$

$\ln Y = 3.05 + 0.0182T + .447\ln Y(-1) + 1.06UMG(-1) + 0.0349\ln G \quad -0.00400\ln MGV - 0.000131\ln MGV(-1)$ (4)
   (4.25)(4.27)   (3.52)   (3.54)   (3.30)   (1.89)   (-0.44)   (-0.16)

$R^2 = 0.998$, SE $= 0.0200$, DW $= 1.67$

$\ln Y = 2.36 + 0.0150T + 0.564\ln Y(-1) + 0.90UMG + 1.00UMG(-1) + 0.0300\ln G \quad -0.0138\ln IRV$ (5)
   (3.61)(3.92)   (4.89)   (3.51)   (3.97)   (2.05)   (-3.02)

$R^2 = 0.998$, SE $= 0.0172$, DW $= 2.23$

$\ln Y = 2.99 + 0.0187T + 0.451\ln Y(-1) + 0.99UMG + 0.86UMG(-1) + 0.0353\ln G \quad -0.0139\ln IRV(-1)$ (6)
   (5.02)(5.21)   (4.25)   (4.07)   (3.41)   (2.48)   (-3.23)

$R^2 = 0.998$, SE $= 0.0170$, DW $= 1.96$

Note: The decimal figures in parentheses are *t* statistics. SE refers to standard error of the regression and DW its Durbin–Watson statistic.

27

- The regression coefficients for the current and last year's interest rate volatilities [*IRV* or *IRV*(-1)] are highly significant by statistical standards (Table 2.1, Equations 5 and 6). The magnitude of the coefficients and the amount that interest rate volatility has changed over time imply that the coefficients are economically significant as well. The rise in interest rate volatility after 1979 probably did contribute to the severity of the recession.

A MODEL OF THE U.S. ECONOMY

Further tests of various combinations of different variables yielded an equation relating unanticipated money growth, real federal purchases of goods and services, interest rate volatility, the previous year's real GNP, and a time trend to the current year's real GNP (Appendix, Equation A1). These empirical results were used to produce an annual model for output in the United States. The Appendix reports the regression equations of that model. Here, it suffices to point out some of its implications.

- Increased interest rate volatility lowers output. For example, doubling interest rate volatility reduces output by 1.44 percent in the first year, 1.50 percent in the second year, and 1.56 percent ultimately.[2] Since interest rate volatility has doubled and, indeed, redoubled since 1978, this effect is economically important.
- Money growth greater than the public has anticipated is associated with appreciably higher output, and money growth less than anticipated is associated with lower output. This effect tends to persist. A one-time unanticipated increase of 1 percentage point in the M1 growth is associated with a 1.05 percent increase in real GNP in the first year, 1.27 percent in the second year, and 0.66 percent more in the third year.[3] Ultimately, there is no increase in the level of real GNP owing to the unanticipated money growth.
- Increasing real federal purchases raises output somewhat.
- When the share of federal purchases in GNP is constant, when there is no unanticipated money growth, and when interest rate volatility is constant, output tends to grow by 3.70 percent per year [3.70 percent = 0.0163/(1 -0.516 -0.0429)].
- Output that is above trend tends to persist—high output in one year tends to be followed by output above trend in later years.

Implications for Recent U.S. Experience

This model is useful for analyzing how the U.S. has behaved since the Federal Reserve changed policy in 1979. Each year since then, real GNP has diverged significantly from its average annual growth rate of 3.7 percent. In terms of this model, both increased interest rate volatility and much slower-than-anticipated money growth contributed to the severity of the 1981–82 recession.

Between 1978 and 1980 interest rate volatility soared (Graph 2.2). Such an increase in interest rate volatility contributed mightily to the stagnation of the U.S. economy. Using 1980 as the base year, the increase in interest rate volatility reduced the level of output cumulatively by 1.88 percent in 1980, 3.87 percent in 1981, 3.64 percent in 1982, and 3.68 percent in 1983 (Appendix, Equation A1).

The implications for growth rates are derived by taking the year-to-year change in the cumulative effects on the level of output. The change in output growth associated with the change in interest rate volatility was -1.88 percent in 1980 (the base year), -1.79 percent in 1981, 0.23 percent in 1982, and -0.04 percent in 1983.

The effect of unanticipated money growth on the economy can be analyzed in a similar fashion. From 1980 through 1982 money growth was below its "anticipated" level. Anticipated money growth is based on a statistical relationship between money growth in the current year and money growth in the prior year, the gap between real federal spending and its normal level, and the employment rate in the previous two years. Unanticipated money growth is the difference (error term) between actual money growth and estimated money growth (Appendix, Equation A2).

Using 1980 as the base year, unanticipated negative money growth reduced the level of output cumulatively by 0.73 percent in 1980 (the base year), 1.04 percent in 1981, and 1.49 percent in 1982. The explosion in unanticipated money growth between 1982 and 1983, however, more than offset the previous three years of unanticipated negative money growth and elevated the level of output on a cumulative basis to 1.08 percent above where it would have been, had money growth remained neutral during the 1980–83 period.

Looking at the year-to-year changes in this cumulative series indicates that unanticipated money growth reduced output growth by 0.73 in 1980, 0.31 percent in 1981, and 0.45 percent in 1982 and increased output growth by 2.57 percent in 1983. By implication, if there had been no unanticipated money growth, the economic recovery would not have gotten off the ground. Instead of growing by 3.42 percent between 1982 and 1983, it would have grown by only 0.84 percent (3.42-2.58 = 0.84).

Over the period of 1980–83, interest rate volatility depressed the level of output nearly six times more on average than did unanticipated money growth. Based on these results, the Federal Reserve can be faulted much more for permitting the high level of interest rate volatility that prevailed between 1979 and 1983 than it can for producing unanticipated money growth, while the volatility in money growth per se had no discernible effect on real GNP growth. In addition, the sharply reduced interest rate volatility experienced in 1983 augured well for the U.S. economy in 1984 and beyond.

Predictive Power of the Model

The model can be used to forecast the level of real GNP: Actual GNP (in 1972 dollars) and the real GNP estimated by the model for the 1947–83 period are plotted in Graph 2.3. Before 1982 these forecasts have reasonable properties. No proportional forecast error exceeds 3.2 percentage points in absolute value; large forecast errors never occur in adjacent years; and there is no tendency for Equation A1 either to overpredict or to underpredict for long periods of time. In contrast, since 1982 forecasted output has been much larger than actual output. Specifically, the estimated real GNP for 1982 and 1983 was 3.8 and 4.1 percentage points, respectively, above actual real GNP.

The model is not alone in forecasting 1982 and 1983 poorly. The most widely marketed econometric models forecasted 1982 and 1983 abominably, too. Something not encompassed by the model of this essay or by the other forecasting models made 1982 and 1983 hard to forecast.

One possible explanation for these large estimation errors is that they do not incorporate the effects of the tax cuts phased in between 1981 and 1984. Lower tax rates in the future created incentives for economic agents to put off producing in 1982 and, to a lesser extent, in 1983. By so doing and also by shifting tax deductions into 1982 and 1983, the present value of an individual's tax liabilities could be reduced. If this explanation has validity, phasing in the Reagan tax cut was folly.

Because of the structure of the model, the estimation errors in 1982 and 1983 by themselves will contribute to a forecast of exceptional growth in 1984. Moreover, since the model is designed to estimate the level of GNP, the forecast of next year's real GNP will be made by definition at the outer limit of the range encompassed by the sample period used to

GRAPH 2.3. Actual and Estimated Real Gross National Product

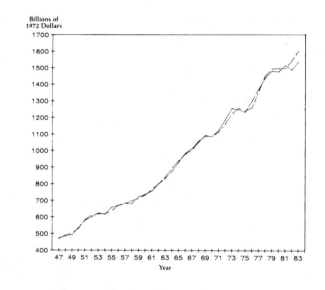

_____ Actual gross national product (1972 dollars).
------ Estimated gross national product (1972 dollars).

Sources: National Income and Product Accounts. U.S. Department of Commerce, Bureau of Economic Analysis. Government Printing Office, Washington D.C.

estimate the coefficients in the model. It is at this outer point that the error terms of any statistical model are most likely to be large and unpredictable.

In order to minimize these sources of error, the 1984 growth rate forecast will be made on the basis of the forecasted level of GNP relative to the model's estimate for 1983 GNP. [The forecast for the 1984 GNP is $1,692.1 billion (1972 dollars), 10.1 percent above the 1983 real GNP of $1,536.9 billion.] For 1985 the growth rate is based on the difference between the estimated level of GNP in 1985 and 1984.

A plot of the year-to-year growth rate in actual real GNP to the implied growth rate based on the estimated level of real GNP suggests the approach should provide a reasonable forecast for real GNP growth. The implied real GNP growth rate in 1983, based on the model's estimates for the level of GNP, for example, was 3.8 percent, compared with the actual growth rate of 3.5 percent.

In addition, several assumptions about 1984 must first be made:[4]

- There will be no unanticipated money growth in 1984 and 1985.
- Because of the military buildup, real federal purchases will rise 1 percent more than real GNP in 1984 and 1985.
- Interest rate volatility in 1984 and 1985 will remain at the 0.22 percent that it averaged during 1983.
- The factors affecting output other than those included in the regression analysis will have a net effect of zero. This assumption excludes any explicit estimation of the growth-augmenting effects of the Reagan tax cut. However, the structure of the model, which anticipates rapid recoveries after severe recessions, may capture their effect indirectly.

Using the forecasting method described, these assumptions and the data available on December 31, 1983, imply that the year-over-year growth in real GNP will be 5.7 percent in 1984 and 4.4 percent in 1985 (Graph 2.4).

The unanticipated explosion of money growth from August 1982 to May 1983 will contribute essentially nothing in 1984 and is forecasted to reduce output growth by nearly 1.9 percent in 1985. The negative effect of the declining positive contribution to real GNP of unanticipated positive money growth is the main reason for the slowdown in real GNP growth between 1984 and 1985.

Given the large error terms in 1982 and 1983, the point estimate for real GNP has to be treated with caution. Nonetheless, the model indicates that economic growth in 1984 may be significantly higher than the consensus forecast.

APPENDIX

The analysis of the text is based on the two regressions below, which were fitted to annual data spanning the period 1947–83:

$$\ln Y = 2.57 + 0.0163T + 0.516 \ln Y(-1) + 1.053 UMG$$
$$\quad (0.69)\ (0.0043)\quad (0.124)\qquad\qquad (0.258)$$

$$+0.731 UMG(-1) + 0.0429 \ln G - 0.0208 \ln IRV(-1) \qquad \text{(A1)}$$
$$\quad (0.275)\qquad\qquad (0.0144)\quad\ (0.0055)$$

$$+0.0099 \ln IRV(-2) + RY,$$
$$\quad (0.0063)$$

GRAPH 2.4. Change in Real Gross National Product, 1947–85

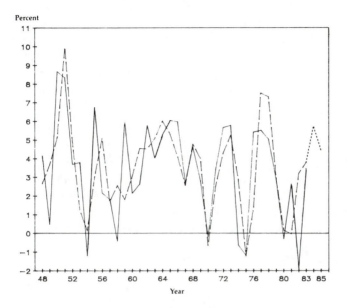

_____ Actual change in real gross national product (1972 dollars).
------ Estimated change in real gross national product.
-------- Forecasted change in real gross national product: 1984–85.

Sources: National Income and Product Accounts. U.S. Department of Commerce, Bureau of Economic Analysis. Government Printing Office, Washington, D.C.

$$R_2 = 0.9977, \; SE = 0.01726, \; DW = 2.07$$

and

$$MG = 0.0560 + 0.712MG(-1) + 0.0721FEDV$$
$$(0.0263) \; (0.093) \qquad\quad (0.0206)$$

$$+ .0460 \ln [U(-1)/1 - U(-1)] - 0.0273 \; \ln [U(-2)/1 - U(-2)] \quad (A2)$$
$$(0.0102) \qquad\qquad\qquad\quad (0.0103)$$

$$+ UMG,$$

$$R_2 = 0.746, \; SE = 0.0127, \; DW = 1.94,$$

where Y is real GNP, T is a time trend, UMG is unanticipated money growth, G is real federal purchases, IRV is interest rate volatility, RY is the residual from Equation A1, MG is the growth rate of the M1 money supply, $FEDV$ is the proportional gap between real federal spending and its normal level,[5] U is the civilian unemployment rate expressed as a fraction, UMG is the residual of Equation A2, and (-1) or (-2) attached to a symbol indicates that it is lagged one or two years, respectively, and DW is the Durbin–Watson statistic. The decimal figures in parentheses are standard errors. Note that unanticipated money growth is defined to be the part of money growth that cannot be predicted using Equation A2, that is, the residual of Equation A2. Note also that the model is monetarist in character and hence does not incorporate any supply-side effects.[6] These were left out not because the author thinks that they are unimportant, but because he wished to show the importance of interest rate volatility and the unimportance of money growth volatility in as monetarist a model as possible.

NOTES

1. For the details of the development of these equations, see Evans (1981).
2. The figures are $0.0208 \ln 2$, $(1.516 \times 0.0208 - 0.0099) \ln 2$, and $[(0.0208 - 0.009)/(1 - 0.516)] \ln 2$.
3. The second and third figures are $1.053 \times 0.516 + 0.731$ and 1.27×0.516.
4. The forecasts are, of course, sensitive to the assumptions they embody, particularly to the estimates for unanticipated money growth and interest rate volatility. Every percentage point of unanticipated money growth in 1984 would indicate a 1.05 percent increment to output this year and a 1.27 percent increment in 1985. If interest rate volatility is another 0.10 higher in 1984 than assumed here, output will be 0.21 percent lower in 1985.
5. More precisely, $FEDV = \ln(FED/FED^*)$. $\ln FED^*$ is a weighted average of current and past values of $\ln FED$ with weights that decay geometrically at the rate of 0.2 per year, and FED equals nominal federal spending divided by the GNP deflator.
6. For a discussion of why unanticipated, and only unanticipated, money growth should affect output, see Lucas (1972), Sargent (1976), and Barro (1976). Barro's 1977 and 1978 articles provide empirical support for this theoretical proposition and also guide one in how to measure unanticipated money growth and what form the equation for output should take. See my previously referenced paper for a more detailed description of how UMB was actually measured.

One can give the term in $\ln G$ a supply-side interpretation. Consider an increase in Federal government purchases. From any given national product, fewer goods and services are available for the private sector. Households may therefore feel poorer. To the extent they do, they make up in part for the fall in their wealth by supplying more factor services to the market economy. In addition, if the increase in G is temporary, they borrow from their relatively richer future, thereby driving up real interest rates. The higher real interest rate in turn makes it more worthwhile to use factor services now when it can earn a high return than in the future when they will not. These effects are offset to the extent that higher marginal tax rates accompany the higher G. The positive coefficient of $\ln G$ suggests that the offset was only partial during the postwar period. For a more complete discussion of these issues, see Barro (1984a, ch. 13–15).

REFERENCES

Barro, R. J. 1984a. *Macroeconomics*. New York: John Wiley & Sons.

——. 1984b. "The Effects on Output of Money-Growth and Interest-Rate Volatility in the United States," *Journal of Political Economy* 92:204–22.

——. 1978. "Unanticipated Money, Output, and the Price Level in the United States," *Journal of Political Economy* 86 (August):549–80.

——. 1977. "Unanticipated Money Growth and Unemployment in the United States," *American Economic Review* 67:101–15.

——. 1976. "Rational Expectations and the Role of Monetary Policy," *Journal of Monetary Economics* 2:1–32.

Evans, P. 1981. "Why Have Interest Rates Been So Volatile?," *Economic Review of the Federal Reserve Bank of San Francisco* (Summer):7–20.

Friedman, B. 1982. "Federal Reserve Policy, Interest Rate Volatility, and the U.S. Capital Raising Mechanism," *Journal of Money, Credit and Banking* 14:721–45.

Friedman, M. 1982a. "An Aborted Recovery?," *Newsweek* 98 (August 23):59.

Friedman, M. 1982b. "The Yo-Yo Economy," *Newsweek* 96 (February 15):72.

Lucas, R. 1972. "Expectations and the Neutrality of Money," *Journal of Economic Theory* 4:103–24.

Meltzer, A. H. 1982. "The Results of the Fed's Failed Experiment," *Wall Street Journal* (July 29):24.

Sargent, T. 1976. "A Classical Macroeconometric Model for the United States," *Journal of Political Economy* 84:207–38.

3

The Price Rule and the Anatomy of a Gold Standard
Charles W. Kadlec and Arthur B. Laffer

SUMMARY

A price rule as the primary guide to the conduct and monitoring of monetary policy is being put into place. It is the final precondition for the "Roaring Eighties." A price rule stabilizes commodity prices within a narrow range and allows the quantity of money to do the adjusting to fluctuations in the demand for money. By contrast, a quantity rule stabilizes the growth rate in the money supply, destabilizing prices and interest rates as the financial markets equilibrate the fluctuations in money demand to an inflexible money supply.

Since 1982 the Federal Reserve has deemphasized stabilizing the growth rate of money, emphasizing instead various indications of economic activity including sensitive commodity prices. Since then, interest rates have declined, equity values have risen, and the relative price of gold has fallen. The economy in 1983 and 1984 posted the strongest expansion since 1951. This surge in growth was accompanied by lower inflation and interest rates.

Full institutionalization of a price rule through an explicit guarantee of the dollar's value, in terms of a basket of commodities or even in terms of a single commodity such as gold, would produce in short order far lower interest rates and, by definition, long-run price stability. With interest rates lower and the value of the dollar secure, the demand for dollars, and hence their quantity, would increase. Real money would rise, and the financial system would reliquefy. The result would be an economic resurgence potentially exceeding any other in the history of the United States. The ripple effects of economic growth at home would stretch across international boundaries, facilitating trade and encouraging a majority of Western nations to fix their currencies to the dollar.

Once again, the modern world would have at its disposal currency or numeraire whose standard of value is accepted across borders as well as over time. Once again workers and consumers, savers and investors, would be able to transact in a common medium of exchange throughout the world and over horizons both distant and near.

THE PRICE RULE

A price rule for monetary policy—the final precondition for the "Roaring Eighties"—is being put into place. It is the successor to the quantity rule—stabilizing the growth rate in the money supply—as the primary guide to the conduct and monitoring of policy. Under a price rule, commodity prices are stabilized within a narrow range. Under a quantity rule, the emphasis has been to stabilize the growth rate in the money supply. Until the full significance of the change to a price rule is incorporated into market behavior, tracking commodity prices can provide opportunities to anticipate correctly movements in interest rates and the stock market.

The choice between a price rule and a quantity rule is one that permeates the day-to-day running of every business. A quantity rule is analogous to a company producing and selling the same number of widgets each and every day. As the demand for widgets fluctuates, the price of widgets will rise and fall. When output is short of demand, prices will be raised to ration the available supply. But when output is in excess of demand, prices will be cut in order to move the product into the market (Figure 3.1a).

Most companies, however, choose instead to stabilize the price of their output. Small fluctuations in demand are accommodated by changes in inventory levels. Larger changes in demand induce changes in the level of production. Within this range, the company will meet any demand at a given price (Figure 3.1b). Only substantial and sustained changes in demand lead to the setting of a new price, at which point the process begins anew. In sum, when quantities are stabilized, prices will fluctuate in order to clear the market. Similarly, if the price at which a commodity is offered is stable, then quantities must do the adjusting. Only these two options exist.

Between 1979 and 1982 the Federal Reserve emphasized targeting the quantity of money. The volatility in interest and inflation rates was

FIGURE 3.1. The Choice between a Quantity Rule and a Price Rule

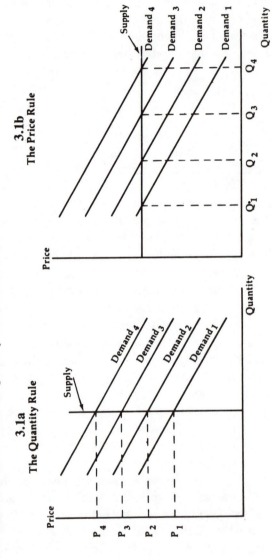

3.1a
The Quantity Rule

3.1b
The Price Rule

Source:·Author's calculations

38

the inevitable consequence. Since 1982 the Fed has deemphasized stabilizing the growth rate of money, choosing instead to monitor various indications of economic activity and inflation, including sensitive commodity prices. Interest rates and commodity prices have become far more stable, but the growth rate of money has become more volatile (Graph 3.1).

The decline in interest rates, the rise in equity values, and the fall in the relative price of gold that coincided with this policy change are remarkable. The economy in 1983 and 1984 posted the strongest expansion since 1951. Yet contrary to the forewarnings of virtually all leading economists, this surge in growth was accompanied by lower inflation and interest rates:

• In 1984 the gross national product (GNP) deflation advanced at a 3.7 percent annual rate (preliminary), down from 6.0 percent in 1982 and 9.6 percent in 1981.

• By December 1984 yields on 30-year government bonds averaged 11.52 percent, compared with a peak of 14.5 percent reached in 1981. Three-month Treasury bill rates averaged 8.06 percent, less than half of the 16.30 record for May 1981.

As impressive as these gains are, interest rates, by any but these kind of comparisons, are unbelievably high. Between 1931 (the first year data are available) and 1965, the market yield on three-month Treasury bills never exceeded 5 percent. Using 90-day prime bankers' acceptance as a proxy, an average rate above 5 percent for a year does not appear until as far back as 1921.

In this context, the height of interest rates that prevailed at the end of 1984 was indicative of a lack of confidence that recent price stability will persist into the future. Simply put, the success in slowing the rate of inflation in 1983 and 1984 has not been translated fully into confidence in the future.

Restoration of a monetary standard would provide this confidence by guaranteeing the value of the dollar in terms of a basket of commodity or even a single commodity such as gold. Simply put, the monetary authority would commit itself to provide as much or as little money to the private economy as participants in the economy desire at a fixed value of money. Such a commitment is the essence of a price rule for monetary policy. It is not gold that is important—it is the standard that matters.

It is not possible to know or forecast the correct amount of money needed to serve the economy. The present system of targeting money supply growth cannot effectively deal with the uncertainty of future economic

GRAPH 3.1. Spot Commodity Index Versus Federal Funds Rate, June 1 to October 8, 1982

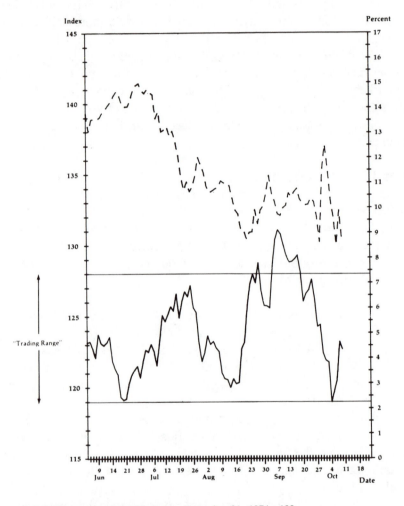

_____Dow Jones spot commodity index, December 31, 1974 = 100.
------Federal funds rate.

Sources: Selected Interest Rates, Federal Reserve Board, Government Printing Office, Washington, D.C.; Wall Street Journal.

events and the resultant shifts in the demand for money. The appropriate growth in money supply is the rate needed by the marketplace to conduct transactions efficiently. With a gold standard, market participants, by exchanging dollars for gold or gold for dollars at a fixed price, control money supply growth. This price rule approach equilibrates the supply of and demand for money by focusing on the value or "quality" of money.

Under a gold standard, when individuals bring dollars to the Treasury for gold, it is an indication that there is an excess amount of dollars. This dollar redemption is an effective signal to the Federal Reserve to reduce the monetary base until individuals are no longer turning in money for gold. Similarly, when individuals bring gold to the Treasury for dollars, the marketplace is signaling a shortage of money. The Federal Reserve response is to inject reserves into the system until the sale of gold to the Treasury ceases. In this way, market participants signal a need for a change in the supply of money. The quantity of money in this way is demand determined at a stable value.

Traditional ideas of a gold standard imply a type of discipline: a stipulated relationship between the amount of gold and the quantity of money. Under a modern-day gold standard, there need not be such a strict relationship. The monetary authority should be concerned with maintaining a quality product rather than stipulating its quantity.

THE IMPACT OF A GOLD STANDARD

While the mechanism for implementing a gold standard is relatively simple, the ramifications are substantial:

- The primary effect will be a reduction in secular inflation, resulting in dramatically lower interest rates.
- A gold standard would also serve to reliquefy the financial system. Since dollars would be as good as gold, a gold standard would restore confidence in the value of currency over the long term.
- A substantial increase in demand for currency and demand deposits would result, leading to substantially higher real money balances. In other words, individuals and corporations will be much more willing to hold dollars when interest rates are low and the future value of the dollar is secure than when interest rates are high and the future of the dollar is uncertain. This increase in real money balances would accommodate either accelerating loan demand or additional purchases of government securities by the banks.

Once the dollar is made as good as gold, there would be little reason to hold foreign currencies, gold, or other inflation hedges as protection against a depreciating dollar. In short order, the purchasing power of gold would diminish, as opposed to the sharp run-up in the purchasing power of gold during the 1970s when the United States abandoned the gold standard.

To understand the full effects of guaranteeing the value of the dollar, imagine for a moment that you and everyone else knew with perfect certainty that one dollar 30 years from now and in all intervening periods would be worth exactly what it is today. If such confidence were to replace today's uncertainty, short-term Treasury bill rates once again would be at 2 percent, the prime rate at 3 percent, and mortgage rates for individuals at 5 percent. The result would be an economic resurgence unparalleled in our history. The devastating legacies of Presidents Johnson, Nixon, Ford, and Carter would finally be put behind us. The housing and auto industries would soar as home mortgage and auto loan rates fall to 6 percent or below. Steel, coal, industrial construction, and many other industries would be quick to follow. With a prime rate of 4 percent, businesses new and old would expand, creating a vast number of new jobs—especially in the nation's depressed areas.

The benefits would be most pronounced for the unemployed, minorities, and disadvantaged. Truck drivers never do well when trucks are not operating. Modernized factories and intellectual acuity are rarely extracted from the ranks of the unemployed, flophouses, or soup kitchens. The ripple effects of economic growth extend far beyond the steel mills and auto factories.

The impact of the restitution of a monetary standard on the fiscal position of the federal government would be as salutary as its effect on the economy. Interest paid annually by the federal government for the national debt now exceeds $137 billion. This expenditure is the third largest item in the budget and, taken alone, is equivalent to 80 percent of the federal deficit.

Since 1977 the federal debt has nearly doubled to $1.4 trillion, and yet interest expenditures have risen three-and-one-half-fold. The difference is the unbelievable increase in interest rates. In 1977 the rate on three-month Treasury bills was 5.3 percent. In recent years the government has paid as much as 12 percent and even 15 percent to borrow money.

At historical interest rates, the cost of financing this $1.4 trillion national debt would, in short order, fall to about $42 billion, thereby eliminating some $95 billion in annual federal interest expenditures.

The positive effects would not stop there. As a rule of thumb, for every one-percentage point reduction in the unemployment rate, the deficit falls by \$25 billion annually. By reducing unemployment to 4 percent, \$75 billion of the deficit would be erased without Congress changing any tax or expenditure programs.

INTERNATIONAL IMPLICATIONS

Reinstatement of dollar/gold convertibility has substantial strategic implications as well:

- The Soviet Union was a substantial seller of gold in the late 1970s at a time when the purchasing power of gold rose by a multiple of ten from 1971. The return to the gold standard would effectively reduce the price of gold, thus reducing the unintended subsidy of the Soviet Union. A similar effect would be felt by gold-producing South Africa.
- A gold standard would reestablish the dollar as the universal currency and thus would make it the choice for international transactions. This event would greatly facilitate international trade and unify the international monetary system.
- Without a well-defined relationship to the dollar, foreign currencies would become a less attractive financial medium. Therefore, it is presumed that the majority of Western nations would fix their currencies to the gold-based dollar and develop appropriately consistent monetary policy. The universal currency would have implications for multinational corporations as well, the most important being the elimination of complex foreign currency transactions.

The transition back to a gold standard is not without risk. As many of the critics of dollar/gold convertibility have pointed out, setting the price too high would mean continued inflation, while establishing a price that is too low would cause a sharp drop in the price level.

Fixing the price of gold is too important to be left to an economist or a politician. The price of dollar convertibility to gold must be set by the marketplace. By allowing the market to set the price, the relationship between the dollar and gold at the time of fixing should be very close to its equilibrium price. This means that during the transition period back to a monetary standard, declines in the price of gold should not be resisted. This is not cause for alarm. Gold is the first refuge of the cautious. High gold prices indicate that something is wrong with the dollar, the economy, or international politics. The lower the price of gold, the better the overall prospects are. During the first year of the Great Depression, the relative price of gold rose sharply. A stable price of gold today at the $400 to $450 range could well mean a lot higher inflation over the years ahead. With the continued strength of the U.S. economic recovery and recent indications that dollar inflation remains under control, the need to hold gold as a hedge has diminished. As a result, it is gold's price, not the general price level, that is in decline.

If the United States is to return to a monetary standard, additional declines in the price of gold can be expected. For example, if the purchasing power of gold, in terms of the Bureau of Labor Statistics All Commodities Index, were to return to its 1949 level—the year the U.S. official gold stock hit its all-time high—the gold price would fall to $138 per ounce. Even if gold's purchasing power were to return to its 1897 level—identified in Professor Roy Jastram's book, *The Golden Constant,* as the pre-Federal Reserve peak—the price of gold would decline to $268 per ounce.

CONCLUSION

A gold standard is only a means to an end—that end being a stable value for money. While gold is not a perfect mechanism to accomplish this end, history demonstrates that a gold standard has been quite effective in removing the uncertainty of unchecked monetary policies that result in ever-higher levels of inflation and interest rates. At present, gold seems the only reasonable alternative to the erratic monetary policies of recent years.

Throughout U.S. history, when the link between dollar and gold is severed, secular inflation appears. When the link is restored, price stability ensues. In 1862 the United States began issuing an unbacked paper currency. Wholesale prices more than doubled within three years. In 1864 alone prices rose by 45 percent. The process of returning the United States to gold convertibility (set at the pre-Civil War conversion ratio) commenced in 1873 and was completed in 1879. Prices returned to their pre-Civil War level.

Inflation did not really return (except for World War I) until Franklin Roosevelt reduced the gold content of the dollar in 1934 and concomitantly prohibited holdings of gold. From 1933 to 1937 inflation averaged

7 percent per year in spite of the fact that unemployment rates ranged between 14 and 25 percent.

In 1944 President Harry Truman reinstated dollar/gold convertibility. In 1946 personal and corporate tax rates were cut. Between 1945 and 1952, private output (real GNP less defense) expanded at an average annual rate of 5.2 percent, the federal budget was in surplus five out of the seven years, Treasury bills ranged between 0.4 and 1.8 percent, and the rate of inflation fell from its post-World War II peak of 20 percent to 0. Think of it in today's context: Inflation was brought under complete control and unemployment never went as high as 6 percent.

A gold standard encourages people to save money, trusting it to retain its value. Trade is encouraged because a price negotiated today will be good tomorrow. Capital investment expands because industry can calculate costs in constant prices. Labor knows today's wage will buy tomorrow's goods.

One by one, the alternatives to a formal price rule are being exhausted. The all-indicators approach currently used by the Federal Reserve Board turns out to be a no-indicators approach, and fear and uncertainty rule the outlook. More and more, it looks as if another step toward full implementation of an explicit commitment to guarantee the future purchasing power of the dollar is the only viable policy response.

It is simply not true that the wherewithal to establish a Bretton Woods-type monetary system is beyond U.S. capabilities. Dollar/gold convertibility can be reinstituted.

REFERENCE

Jastram, Roy W. 1977. *The Golden Constant.* New York: John Wiley and Sons.

4

Monetary Policy and the Economy: A Neoclassical View
Victor A. Canto and Charles W. Kadlec

SUMMARY

The results of the monetary experiment of the last decade provide new insights into the short-run effects of monetary policy on interest rates, the price level, equity values, and economic growth. Monetary policy produces real economic effects by altering the efficiency of the banking system in its role of supplying credit to the economy. The result is a change in the relative price of credit and hence the real rate of interest. The greater the divergence of the real rate of interest from its long-run equilibrium level, the greater the distortion in credit markets and the greater the loss in economic efficiency and output.

This neoclassical framework explains not only the coincidence of record-high real interest rates and slowing inflation that marked the 1979–82 recessionary period, but also the coincidence of record-low real interest rates and accelerating inflation that marked the 1974–75 recession. It also is consistent with movements in interest rates and the collapse in economic activity that coincided with the imposition of credit controls in 1980 and the timing of the surge in economic activity during the current recovery.

Three major implications emerge from this research:

1. Divergence of the real rate of interest from its long-run equilibrium level, whether above or below, detracts from economic growth.
2. Convergence of the real rate of interest with its long-run equilibrium level, again whether above or below, augments economic growth.
3. A key component of an optimal monetary policy is an implementation of procedures that stabilize the real rate of interest at its long-run equilibrium level.

Investment implications include the following:

1. The decline in the real rate of interest from its 1982 peak has added impetus to the economic recovery and has stimulated above-average growth in corporate profits.
2. A further decline in the real rate of interest, with stabilization between 1 and 3 percent, would augment economic growth.
3. If real rates decline further, those sectors most intensive in the use of credit and therefore most affected by distortions in the credit markets will continue to lead the recovery.

MONETARY POLICY AND THE ECONOMY

The last decade has been a period of radical change in the conduct of monetary policy. The system of fixed exchange rates and dollar/gold convertibility yielded to floating exchange rates and monetary experimentation. Depreciation of the dollar was encouraged until November 1978, when President Jimmy Carter reversed his administration's policy of "benign neglect" of the dollar and committed it to working with other industrial countries, especially Germany and Japan, in stabilizing the value of the dollar.

Within a year, however, it was clear that this approach was not leading to lower U.S. inflation but to a return to a higher rate of inflation in Europe and Japan.[1] By the summer of 1979, inflation was accelerating around the world. Once again, the Europeans and the Japanese threatened to abandon their efforts to stabilize the value of the dollar unless U.S. inflation was reduced quickly. As a result, in October 1979 Federal Reserve Board Chairman Paul Volcker embarked upon a policy of targeting the growth rates in the narrowly defined quantity of money M1 (see Kadlec and Laffer 1979).

The most surpising—and troubling—result of this new policy was the rise in the real rate of interest (short-term interest rates minus the rate of inflation) to levels not seen on a sustained basis since the Greenback Era of 1864–79. More than anything else, it was this increase in the real rate—and symmetrically the surprising low real rates of the mid-1970s— that pushed the relationships between money, credit, interest rates, inflation, and the real economy outside the range of previous experience.

The results of the monetary experiment of the last decade provide new insights into the short-run effects of monetary policy on interest rates, the price level, equity values, and economic growth. These experiences, combined with the brief experience with credit controls in 1980, have led to a reformulation of our basic view of the importance of monetary policy to short-run fluctuations in real economic growth: Monetary policy produces real economic effects by altering the efficiency of the banking system in its role of supplying credit to the economy. The manifestation of these distortions is elevation or suppression of the real rate of interest. Furthermore, the use of long-term, steady-state relationships in the analysis of monetary policy is inappropriate during a transition period from high inflation and interest rates to low inflation and interest rates.

TRADITIONAL CONCEPTS

In the simple Keynesian construct, increasing the supply of money (easy money) will produce an increase in the dollar price of bonds and a commensurate fall in interest rates. Whether inflation accelerates in the Keynesian model or stays the same, as is the case with the original Keynesian model, such a decline in nominal interest rates implies a fall in the real interest rate as well. The fall in the real rate of interest in turn stimulates investment, aggregate demand, and hence overall output. Conversely, decreasing the supply of money (tight money) increases interest rates, elevates the real rate of interest, retards investments, and subtracts from economic growth.

For the monetarist, an increase in the quantity of money also leads to lower nominal interest rates—bond prices rise. Albeit through a somewhat expanded process, an increase in the supply of money still elicits an increase in output and employment. The supply of goods and services merely accommodates the increase in aggregate demand flowing from excessive money balances created by the monetary authorities. In due course, the increased production of goods and services will lead to heightened wage demands and tendencies on the part of goods and services producers to raise prices. Inflation will be the end result. Here, again, in the short run, monetary expansion leads to lower real interest rates and expanded production (see Friedman 1968).

With tight money, demand is initially retarded via an elevation of interest rates and through the direct effect of insufficient money in the hands of consumers. The supply of goods and services declines in response to this decrease in aggregate demand, and the economy contracts as real interest rates rise.

A NEOCLASSICAL VIEW OF MONETARY POLICY

Thus, Keynesians and monetarists agree that an increase in the real interest rate above its long-run equilibrium rate will retard investment and thereby economic growth. In both models, a restriction on monetary growth (tight money) restricts the availability of credit as well, driving up its price. Such a quantity restriction is analogous to a quota. This type of distortion can be illustrated by elevating the real rate of interest above its long-run equilibrium rate determined by the intersection of the supply of capital, or savings, and the demand for capital, or investment (Figure 4.1a). Credit markets clear, but at a lower level of investment, savings, and economic activity. While higher real rates may encourage savings it is of little consequence when those who would otherwise borrow the money are unwilling to do so at the now-higher interest rates.

Contrary to the Keynesian and monetarist formulation, Figure 4.1 also suggests that a decline in the real rate, below its equilibrium level, will retard economic growth. This type of distortion can be illustrated by depressing the real rate of interest below its long-run equilibrium rate (Figure 4.1b). Once again, credit markets clear at a lower level of savings, investment, and economic activity. The reduction in the real rate of interest, below its equilibrium level, may increase investment opportunities. But, at the now-lower rates, a lesser amount of savings is forthcoming. Absent the savings, the desire to increase investments is for naught. Just as with higher real rates, lower real rates would be expected to be associated with lower investment and economic activity (Figure 4.1b).

The point is that when prices are forced to diverge from their undistorted equilibrium level, the first curve to be intersected by the new price determines the level of output—whether it be the demand (elevated real rates of interest) or the supply (depressed real rates of interest) curve. Both artificial increases in price—say, through monopolies, quotas, or taxes—and artificial reductions in price—say, through price controls—reduce production and the general level of output.

There is little disagreement that the historically high real interest rates experienced in the first three years of this decade retarded economic growth. Equally interesting is that the very low real rates of interest during the mid- and late 1970s also were associated with a slowing of economic activity (Graph 4.1). When the real rate of interest deviates significantly from its natural long-run rate, be it above or below, it is symptomatic of a condition of disequilibrium in the nation's credit markets. The resulting misallocation of resources retards economic growth.

This conclusion is supported by the relationship between movements in the stock market and deviations in the real rate from its mean. For the period 1970–82 deviations in the real rate from its average rate for the period were associated with declines in the rate of growth in real gross national product (GNP). A similar negative and statistically significant

FIGURE 4.1. Savings and Investment When Real Interest Rates Are Above or Below Their Equilibrium Level

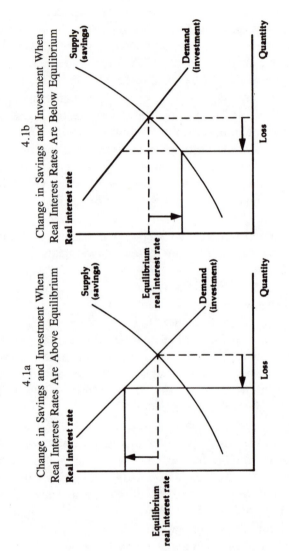

4.1a

Change in Savings and Investment When Real Interest Rates Are Above Equilibrium

4.1b

Change in Savings and Investment When Real Interest Rates Are Below Equilibrium

Source: Author's calculations

50

GRAPH 4.1. The Real Rate of Interest and Economic Growth

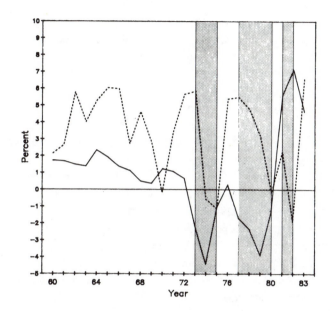

_____ Real interest rate (the average of quarterly real interest rates estimated by the difference between the yield on a three-month Treasury bill at the end of the previous quarter and the annual rate of change in the seasonally adjusted consumer price index for the current quarter).

------ Percentage change in real gross national product.

Periods of substantial divergence of the real rate from its mean.

Sources: Selected Interest Rates, Federal Reserve Board. Government Printing Office, Washington, D.C.; *National Income and Product Accounts,* U.S. Department of Commerce, Bureau of Economic Analysis. Government Printing Office, Washington, D.C.

relationship is found between deviations in the real rate from its mean and the Standard and Poor's 500 Index. Though the R^2 values for these relationships are low, it is nonetheless remarkable that this single variable taken in isolation has significant explanatory power for movements in the economy and stock market.

The Essential Elements

The neoclassical framework developed in this analysis is consistent with the experience that distortions in the real rate of interest—be they positive or negative—are associated with a deterioration in economic performance. It employs many of the basic principles of tax and microeconomic theory.[2] Monetary policy is examined in terms of its ability to distort the banking system and thereby the relative price of credit.

There are three elements essential to the analysis:

1. The imposition of non-interest-bearing reserve requirements on the banking system is equivalent to a tax. The level of bank reserves determines the proportion of the banking system's assets subject to the tax and is thereby analogous to the tax base. The level of interest rates is analogous to the tax rate. Holding reserve requirements constant, the higher the nominal rate of interest, the higher the effective tax rate (Kadlec and Laffer 1979).

The legal requirement to pay below-market interest rates on demand accounts also represents a tax on money holdings equivalent to the difference between the legal maximum rate and the rate the market would bear. To the extent that such a requirement is binding and cannot be offset by "free" bank services, the requirement represents a real penalty on assets held in the form of money narrowly defined. Once again, the higher the market interest and inflation rates, the higher the effective tax rate on demand and other deposits subject to interest rate ceilings.

2. Since competition exists that does not incur the reserve "tax," such as commercial paper, the very existence of banks indicates that they play a unique role in intermediating between short-term lenders and borrowers.[3]

3. Errant monetary policy can create distortions in the banking system. The source of the distortion can emanate from the monetary authority's regulatory powers—such as credit controls—or from its power over the growth rate of the monetary base and thereby its influence over the availability of bank reserves. An increase in the spread between the interest rate paid by users of bank credit and interest rates received by depositors would evidence such a distortion and consequent loss in efficiency of the banking system. Because of the banking system's unique role in the credit markets, such distortions can affect the relative price of credit and hence the real rate of interest. The greater the divergence of the real rate from its long-run equilibrium level, the greater the distortion in the credit markets and the greater the loss in economic efficiency and output.

The neoclassical view of monetary policy suggests that traditional models of Fed policy understate the importance of monetary policy to short-run fluctuations in real economic growth. Credit is a vital ingredient in the operation of the economy. In many respects, short-term credit plays the role of an essential raw material. It is used by companies to improve the efficiency and profitability of their operations. The importance of the efficient production of credit to the economy is captured by the nomenclature—credit crunch—used to describe periods when credit markets have been disturbed.

Thus, monetary policy's impact on the economy does not lie solely in its ability to affect the amount of money in people's pockets. Of far greater importance is its impact on the banking sector's ability to provide its intermediary services to suppliers and demanders of credit.

Regulation Q

The ability of the Federal Reserve to disrupt the banking system originates in its regulatory powers and its influence over the availability of reserves to the banking system. During the 1960s and 1970s, a major source of disturbance was Regulation Q (Reg Q) ceilings on interest that banks could pay on deposits. Reg Q is nothing more than a form of price control, irrelevant until it becomes binding and then profoundly destructive. In this case, the intersection of the maximum interest rate permitted and the supply curve determines the quantity of credit (Figure 4.1b).

In 1966, for example, market rates of interest exceeded Reg Q limits on bank certificates of deposit (CDs). As a result, banks were faced with the likely inability to retain a large precentage of their deposit base. Bank lending came to an abrupt halt and economic activity slowed. A financial crisis loomed. The credit crunch was ended when the Federal Reserve injected reserves (through the monetary base) into the banking system and market rates of interest declined below the Reg Q ceiling. Nevertheless, the potential for crisis had been so great that Reg Q ceilings on large bank CDs subsequently were abolished (see Wojnilower 1980).

Similarly, in the mid-1970s, Reg Q ceilings on savings accounts at thrift institutions brought mortgage lending to a virtual halt. So widespread were the effects that the arcane word "disintermediation" became part of household parlance and journalistic prose. Once again, the effects were so deleterious that the binding effect of Reg Q ceilings was alleviated by allowing thrift institutions and banks to offer depository instruments that paid money market-related interest rates (Wojnilower 1980).

Yet another form of distortion—this time originating within the credit markets themselves—occurred in 1970 when the Penn Central Transportation Company went bankrupt and defaulted on its commercial paper. In the aftermath of this shock, other corporations found it difficult, if not impossible, to roll over their own outstanding commercial paper and, as a result, drew down on their bank standby lines of credit. The banks in turn issued CDs to fund the loans. In essence, little had changed except the banks intermediated between lender and borrower, replacing the commercial paper outstanding with CDs. The one difference—that the bank CDs carried reserve requirements—meant, however, that the existing reserve base of the banking and monetary system was inadequate. A massive credit crunch threatened but was averted as the Fed stepped in and supplied reserves to the banking system.

Credit Controls

Perhaps the most dramatic example of the power of monetary policy to affect the short-run path of the economy was the imposition of credit controls during the second quarter of 1980. In March 1980 reserve requirements were raised to 10 from 8 percent on increases in the "managed liabilities" of banks. Managed liabilities included large CDs and Eurodollars. Equally important, reserve requirements were extended beyond member banks to include nonmember banks, thrift institutions, and money market funds. The stated purpose of these regulations was to slow inflation by inhibiting the growth of credit.

The banking industry responded to this tax increase on its raw material input (higher marginal reserve requirements) and to a limit on its total volume of business as any industry might:

- During April 1980, as credit controls became effective, the price paid by users of bank credit (the prime rate) went up.
- At the same time, the price received by suppliers of credit (the three-month CD rate) went down (Graph 4.2).

In May and June of that year, the spread between the prime rate and the CD rate remained at historic levels even as overall interest rates declined. For the second quarter, the spread between the prime and three-month CD rates tripled to 4.85 percentage points, a quarterly average not seen before or since (Graph 4.2).

This perturbation was transmitted throughout the economy because the higher reserve requirements were placed on increases in the liabilities of money market funds, thrifts, foreign bank branches and agencies,

GRAPH 4.2. Yield on Three-Month Certificates of Deposit and the Prime Rate (Monthly 1979:1–1983:10)

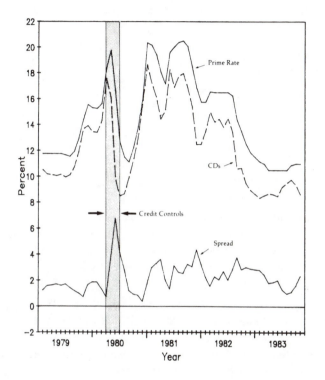

_____ Average bank prime rate.
------ Average yield on three-month certificates of deposit (CDs).
_____ The average prime rate minus the average yield on three-month certificates of deposit.

Source: Selected Interest Rates, Federal Reserve Board. Government Printing Office, Washington, D.C.

Eurodollar deposits, and all other financial intermediaries that could be identified by the Fed. The economic results were startling. During the second quarter of 1980,

- Bank loans, which had been rising at a 13.6 percent annual rate, declined at a 9.3 percent annual rate.
- Extensions of consumer installment credit fell by 22.2 percent.
- The economy contracted at a 9.9 percent annual rate.

As anticipated by the neoclassical view of monetary policy, those parts of the economy most intensive in the use of credit led the contraction. For example, during the second quarter, housing starts were off 16.6 percent and production of durable goods declined by 8.7 percent. Production of nondurable goods fell by only 1.5 percent.

In July the first-month credit controls were eliminated, the prime rate went down, while yields on three-month CDs rose, narrowing the spread from 4.14 percent in June to 2.83 percent in July (Graph 4.2). Economic growth resumed, with real GNP posting a 2.4 percent annual rate of gain in the third quarter.

Tight Money

The Federal Reserve also can affect the capacity of banks to extend credit through open market operations. For example, when the Fed buys bonds in the open market, it increases the monetary base, which in turn increases the potential for credit expansion (Canto and Laffer 1985). The availability of bank reserves is important to the credit markets because reserves are part and parcel of an increase in bank deposits. Absent an increase in deposits, banks in general cannot increase loans. A constraint on increases in the monetary base ultimately constrains the banking system's ability to accept deposits and hence its ability to expand credit.

There is a way to expand credit when reserves are in short supply. To the extent that depositors can be persuaded to switch from high reserve-intensive demand deposits to lower reserve-intensive time deposits, more dollars of loans can be created for every dollar of reserves. Borrowers, however, must be willing to pay depositors to do without the convenience of demand deposits, go through the effort of purchasing time certificates, or pool their deposits in money market mutual funds to buy large CDs. This "payment" would evidence itself in an elevation in the nominal rate of interest above where it otherwise would have been. If inflation were slowing, this could mean nominal interest rates simply remained high instead of declining as well. In any case, this added payment would manifest itself as a higher real rate of interest, which ultimately restores balance between the supply and demand for credit. In this case, the intersection of the now-higher interest rates and the demand curve determines the quantity of credit (Figure 4.1a).

The period of restrictive monetary policy that existed from the fourth quarter of 1980 to the second quarter of 1982 exemplifies this form of disturbance in the credit markets. Inflation, as measured by the consumer price index (CPI), peaked in the first quarter of 1980 at 17.1 percent. During the fourth quarter of that year, inflation averaged 13.4 percent, and by the fourth quarter of 1981 it averaged just 5.4 percent. In March 1982 consumer prices declined for the first time since 1964. Though the CPI returned to double-digit levels in May and June 1982, between December 1981 and December 1982 it advanced by only 3.9 percent, less than half of its 1981 advance and its smallest increase since 1972. This decline in inflation corresponded to a reduction in the rate of growth in the monetary base and a strong dollar policy by the new Reagan administration (Kadlec 1981).

At first, interest rates did not decline; yields on three-month Treasury bills peaked in May 1981 at 16.3 percent and averaged 15.05 percent in the third quarter of that year, 170 basis points higher than their average during the first quarter of 1980. By the second quarter of 1982, however, yields on three-month Treasury bills had declined to 12.42 percent.

This decline in inflation and eventual decline in interest rates were equivalent to a massive tax cut on the banking system. Banks would be expected to become more competitive relative to commercial paper and other forms of nonbank intermediaries. The reduction in the opportunity cost of holding demand and other checkable deposits subject to interest rate ceilings would lead to a shift into these deposits. As a result, the growth rate in the stock of narrowly defined money would be expected to accelerate (Kadlec and Laffer 1979).

This incipient acceleration in the growth rate of the narrowly defined money, however, was at odds with the Federal Reserve's strategy of containing the growth rate in M1. By not accommodating this shift in the demand for reserve-intensive bank liabilities, the Fed, in essence, reduced the monetary base below its equilibrium level and created a shortage of bank reserves.

Once again, the banking system responded in accordance with the neoclassical approach to monetary policy. In essence, the banking system was faced with a quota on a raw material input—reserves—which is necessary for the production of bank loans.

An initial response was evident in the last quarter of 1980, when the spread between market rates on three-month CDs and three-month Treasury bills increased to an average of 2.15 from 0.8 percentage points. Such an increase suggests the banking industry was bidding up the price of low reserve-intensive time deposits as a means of increasing the volume of total deposits and hence credit that could be supported by a dollar of reserves. During that quarter, the prime rate also rose but by less than the increase in the rate paid on three-month CDs. As a result, the spread between the average prime rate and the average three-month CD rate narrowed to 0.97 percentage point (Graph 4.3). Beginning with the first quarter of 1981, this difference increased to an average of 3.29 percentage points. For the years 1980, 1981, and 1982, the average difference between the price paid by users of bank credit (the prime rate) and the suppliers of bank credit (CD rate) increased substantially above where it had been during the previous decade. The same was true for the average spread between the rate paid on three-month CDs and Treasury bills (Graph 4.4).

The increase in the spread between the prime and three-month CD rates indicates that users of bank credit had no readily available substitute. As a result, the shortage of bank reserves was binding on the economy. The increase in the spread between three-month CDs and Treasury bills indicates that the two are not perfect substitutes and that, as good as they are, money market funds and other forms of time deposits are far from perfect substitutes for checking accounts.

The dynamics of the banking system's response to a shortage of reserves combined with the proximate monetary policy goal of limiting the growth in M1 acted to prolong this period of tight money. The switch to time deposits from demand deposits induced by the premiums paid on CDs simply reduced the growth rate of M1 below where it otherwise would have been. This by-product of the credit crunch facilitated achievement of attaining the lower M1 growth targets, indicating to those using this policy goal that monetary policy remained on an appropriate path.

Furthermore, during this period, innovative forms of avoiding the quota on reserves were effectively precluded by the Bank Depository Institutions Deregulation and Monetary Control Act of 1980. It extended non-interest-bearing reserve requirements to all "transaction accounts." That closed the burgeoning loophole for banks that were not members of the Federal Reserve System and therefore not required to maintain non-interest-bearing reserves. It also ended the threat of a wholesale abandonment of the Federal Reserve System by member banks in favor of state charters. Just as important, this law empowered the Board of Governors of the Federal Reserve to determine, by regulation or order, that an account or deposit is a transaction account and thereby subject to reserve requirements.[4]

That provision all but eliminated incentives for money market funds or other potential intermediaries outside the purview of the reserve requirements to create a more convenient, and therefore less expensive, sub-

GRAPH 4.3.   Average Yield on Three-Month Certificates of Deposit and the Prime Rate (Quarterly 1970:1–1983:3)

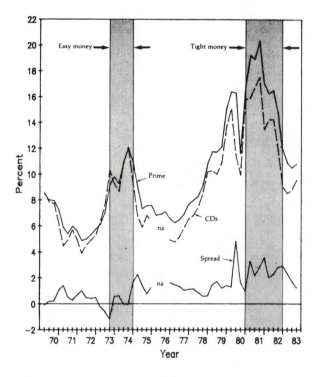

_____ Average bank prime rate.
------ Average yield on three-month certificates of deposit (CDs).
_____ The average prime rate minus the average yield on three-month certificates of deposit.
na: not available.

Source: Selected Interest Rates, Federal Reserve Board. Government Printing Office, Washington, D.C.

stitute for bank demand deposits. With the Fed's grip on the financial system secure, the commitment to slowing the growth rate in the monetary aggregates became binding on the supply of bank reserves and credit as well. Real interest rates—estimated by the difference between the yield on three-month Treasury bills at the end of the previous quarter and the annual rate of change in the seasonally adjusted CPI during the current

GRAPH 4.4. Average Yield on Three-Month Treasury Bills and Three-Month Certificates of Deposit (Quarterly 1970:1–1983:3)

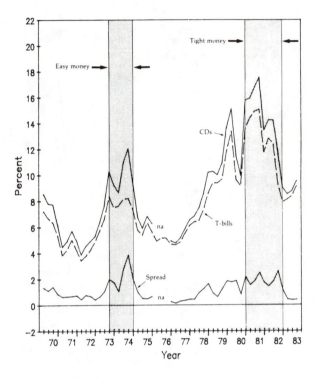

_____ Real interest rate (estimated by the difference between the yield on three-month Treasury bills at the end of the previous quarter and the annual rate of change in the Consumer Price Index during the current quarter).

------ Quarterly change in the seasonally adjusted Consumer Price Index at annual rates.

_____ Secondary market rate on 3-month Treasury bills (bank discount basis) lagged one month.

Sources: "The Consumer Price Index," Bureau of Labor Statistics. Government Printing Office, Washington, D.C.; *Selected Interest Rates,* Federal Reserve Board. Government Printing Office, Washington, D.C.

quarter—rose to a peak of 9.86 percent in the first quarter of 1982, contributing mightily to the depth and length of the 1981–82 recession.

Easy Money

Similar distortions are evident during the period of easy money and negative real rates in the mid-1970s. As inflation and interest rates in the

1971–74 period rose, the effective tax rate on bank reserves and idle balances held in demand deposits also rose. This increase in the effective tax rate set off a chain of events that led to lower real interest rates and significant distortions in the banking system.

In this case, the source of distortion arises out of tax avoidance itself. The existence of persistent market yields on investments well below the "market rate of return" is frequently associated with tax avoidance. An obvious case is the lower yields accepted by investors on tax-exempt municipal bonds relative to yields available on taxable corporate bonds of equal risk and maturity. Similarly, the observable pretax rate of return on tax shelters is negative, while, on an after-tax basis, returns to the taxpayer are positive. In both cases, tax avoidance has the effect of increasing the supply of savings available at any given real rate of return—which shifts the supply curve to the right—producing a new, "below-market" interest rate (Figure 4.2). This distortion, too, leads to an inefficient allocation of capital and impairs overall economic growth.

The notion of a "tax avoidance"-induced distortion is consistent with the observed negative real interest rates of the mid-1970s. In this case, tax avoidance took the form of holders of money balances minimizing the cost of the now-higher bank tax by shifting deposits from reserve-intensive demand deposits to less reserve-intensive time deposits. This shift to less

FIGURE 4.2. How Tax Avoidance Lowers the Observed Pretax Rate of Return

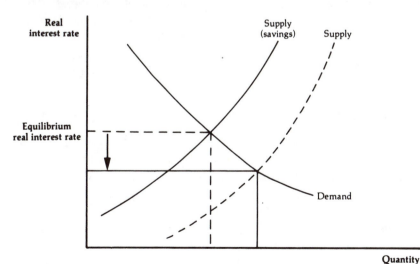

Source: Author's calculations

reserve-intensive CDs also meant that the banking system's capacity to expand credit was increased. But because of the curtailment of investment and other economic activity in the face of inflation and higher taxes, traditional demand for credit shrank.

For banks, the absolute level of interest rates is of far less consequence than the spread between what they charge for loans and what they pay for deposits. Faced with a shrinking loan demand and burgeoning credit capacity, the banking system would have been expected to reduce the price it charged borrowers and depositors until the credit markets were equilibrated. The real rate of interest would have fallen (Figure 4.2). For depositors, accepting negative rates of return was the least costly response in the face of the then-higher effective tax rate on money holdings and bank reserves. Moreover, at the negative real rate, credit demand for purchasing antiques, land, commodities, and other inflation hedges would have been expected to increase.

Between the fourth quarter of 1972 and the first quarter of 1974, the real rate of interest fell to -6.19 from .046 percent, and remained at historically low negative levels through the end of 1974 (Graph 4.5). During this period, the spread between the prime and CD rates collapsed, hitting an average of -1.15 percentage points during the third quarter of 1973 (Graph 4.5). Total bank credit grew at a very rapid rate relative to the quantity of demand deposits and currency in circulation. The negative spread between the prime and CD rates suggests an extreme distortion in the banking system existed. One possible explanation is that the banks were constrained in increasing the prime rate by the threat of price controls or other regulatory restrictions. In any event, during the fourth quarter of 1974 and the first quarter of 1975, the spread between the prime and CD rates increased sharply. The record coincident liquidation of inventories made the 1974–75 recession one of the worst on record.

The Transition Period

The sudden fall in interest rates in July 1982 that accompanied the Fed's decision to deemphasize the monetary aggregates in setting policy suggests the end of the credit crunch and distortions in the financial markets that marred the 1979–82 period. A huge barrier to commerce in the vital credit creation industry was, at least temporarily, reduced.

The rapid increase in the quantity of money evident between June 1982 and August 1983 was a natural result of the easing of the Fed's tight money posture. In effect, the Fed accommodated the already-extant de-

GRAPH 4.5. Inflation, Interest Rates, and the Real Rate of Interest

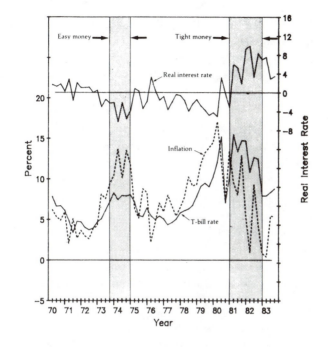

_____ Real interest rate (estimated by the difference between the yield on 3-month Treasury bills
          at the end of the previous quarter and the annual rate of change in the Consumer Price Index
          during the current quarter).
------- Quarterly change in the seasonally adjusted Consumer Price Index at annual rates.
_____ Secondary market rate on 3-month Treasury bills (bank discount basis) lagged one month.

Sources: "The Consumer Price Index," Bureau of Labor Statistics. Government Printing Office,
Washington, D.C.; *Selected Interest Rates,* Federal Reserve Board. Government Printing Office,
Washington, D.C.

mand for money, relieving the artificial restraints on holdings of liquid
balances in the form of currency and demand deposits. The consequent
M1 growth at annual rates in excess of 10 percent was not per se inflationary. Comparison of the relationship between nominal GNP growth and
M1 that existed in 1976 and at the end of this year's third quarter indicates that, if inflation were to remain below 3 percent and short-term interest rates were to decline to between 5 and 7 percent, one or more additional years of 10 percent growth in M1 would be unavoidable. In 1976

every dollar in the narrowly defined money supply turned over 5.5 times. To restore that relationship would require a one-time, 16 percent increase in M1 relative to nominal GNP.

Identifying the end of the transition period is of critical importance to the conduct of monetary policy. At that point, the "rules of the game" will change just as surely as they changed when inflation and interest rates began to fall. As the transition ends, it is possible that real interest rates may fall abruptly as impediments to bank intermediation are eliminated.

Once individuals and businesses have completed their shift of liquid balances back into currency and checking accounts, the monetary base and M1 once again should grow on average at the long-run nominal growth rate in the economy. Substantial variations in M1 growth rates on a month-to-month or even quarter-to-quarter basis may be evident. As long as interest rates and prices remain relatively stable, such volatility most likely will be due to shifts in the public's demand for money and should be of little concern.

Characteristics of the end of a transition period include the following:

1. M1 and M2 grow at the same rate. Equal growth rates by these two measures of the monetary aggregates will indicate that the shift of liquid balances held in "near monies" into the narrowly defined money supply has been completed, marking the end of this source of rapid money growth.
2. Bank credit and M1 grow at the same rate. Growth in total bank loans equal to or slightly greater than growth in M1 is indicative of equilibrium being restored in the banking sector, thereby eliminating the distortions in money and credit markets.
3. The real rate of interest generally lies between 0 and 3 percent. At this point, the real rate will have returned to its long-run equilibrium rate, suggesting the end of the credit crunch.
4. The ratio of M1 to nominal GNP (velocity) stabilizes. Stable velocity indicates that the demand for money relative to the volume of transactions has stabilized, signaling the end of the shift back into narrowly defined money, M1.

The end of a transition period can occur at various levels of inflation and interest rates. For example, with interest rates and inflation now little different from their year-ago levels, velocity would be expected to stabilize. A further decline in interest rates would mark the beginning of another transition period and velocity once again would fall.

On the other hand, a shift toward monetary instability would foment a different kind of transition period. In this case, inflation and interest rates would rise, velocity would increase, and M1 would grow more slowly than M2.

ECONOMIC AND INVESTMENT IMPLICATIONS

1. The easing of the credit crunch was a key to the economic recovery. Beginning with the second quarter of 1983, the real rate of interest[5] declined to near 3 percent from more than 7 percent, and spreads between the prime, CD, and Treasury bill rates returned to normal levels (Graphs 4.3 to 4.5). With the restoration of the efficiency of the banking system, growth accelerated in those sectors most dependent upon credit, such as autos, consumer durables, home building, and capital goods. A further decline in the real rate of interest to around 2 percent would be associated with continued above-average performance by these credit-intensive sectors during the coming year.

2. The creation of money market deposit accounts (MMDAs) with zero-reserve requirements for individuals and 3 percent reserve requirements for corporations eases the threat of future credit crunches. MMDAs offer a more convenient (lower-cost) substitute than money market mutual funds for high reserve-intensive checking accounts. Because of their zero-reserve requirements, MMDAs increase the elasticity of the banking system's deposit base for a given level of reserves. Thus, for a given increase in interest rates or inflationary expectations, more money would be expected to be switched out of reserve-intensive demand accounts to zero-reserve MMDAs. Growth rates in M1 would slow, the effects of the "reserve tax" would be mitigated, and the banking system would be able to continue to intermediate between depositor and borrower with little loss in efficiency. As a result, the real rate of interest could decline even though interest and inflation rates remained high. The more perfect MMDAs are as a substitute for demand accounts, the smaller the loss in efficiency as the banking system responds to changes in reserves, and the lower the cost to the economy of errant Federal Reserve policy.

3. Banks and thrift institutions (savings and loans, savings banks, etc.) will increase their share of the credit markets. First, lower inflation and interest rates are equivalent to a tax cut for the banking industry. This "tax cut" should lead to a decrease in the spread between the price paid for bank credit and the interest rate received by bank depositors. This alone would permit banks to capture a greater share of deposits and loans from alternative sources of credit, including the commercial paper market and Eurodollar markets.

Second, the competitiveness of banks and thrift institutions relative to money market funds and commercial paper has been enhanced by the creation of Super Now accounts, which, with a $2,500 minimum balance, pay a market rate of interest to individuals (not corporations). The creation of MMDAs, which pay market rates of interest, are quite liquid, and have zero-reserve requirements (for individuals), also will enhance the competitiveness of banks and thrift institutions.

4. Money market mutual funds will lose market share to bank MMDAs. As a result, money market mutual funds can be expected to expand the market for commercial paper. Commercial paper, like MMDAs, has no reserve requirements.

5. The rate of growth in M1 will tend to be above its long-run trend rate until the transition from the high-inflation and high-interest rate environment of the 1970s to zero-inflation and low-interest rate environment is over. The recent slowing of M1 growth is consistent with the recent rises in inflation and interest rates. Further reductions in inflation and interest rates would be expected to produce another spate of fast money growth. Once this transition ends, M1 growth rates again would be in approximate proportion to nominal GNP growth rates.

NOTES

1. For an analysis of the effects of exchange rate systems on the balance of payments and world inflation, see Laffer (1974).

2. For a summary of the disincentive effects of taxation, see Canto et al. (1983).

3. If the two sources of credit were perfect substitutes, banks would bear the full burden of the "tax." The tax also would reduce the level of bank activities, which would be largely offset by other forms of credit. See Laffer (1970, 1974).

4. Bank Depository Institutions Deregulation and Monetary Control Act of 1980, Public Law 96-221 (March 31, 1980).

5. For purposes of this calculation, the real rate of interest is defined as the difference between the yield on three-month Treasury bills at the end of the previous quarter and the annual rate of change in the seasonally adjusted CPI during the current quarter.

REFERENCES

Canto, Victor A., Douglas Joines, and Arthur B. Laffer (eds.). 1983. *Foundations of Supply-Side Economics*. New York: Academic Press.

Canto, Victor A., and Arthur B. Laffer. 1985. "Can the Fed Control the Money Supply?" A. B. Laffer Associates, Lomita, CA (forthcoming).

Friedman, Milton. 1968. "The Role of Monetary Policy," *American Economic Review* Vol. 58, No.1 (March): 1–17.

Kadlec, Charles W. 1981. "A New Monetary Policy," A. B. Laffer Associates, Lomita, CA (March).

Kadlec, Charles W., and Arthur B. Laffer. 1979. "The Monetary Crisis: A Classical Perspective," A. B. Laffer Associates, Lomita, CA (November).

Laffer, Arthur B. 1974. "Trade Credit and Other Forms of Inside Money," presented at the Stanford Conference honoring Edward Shaw (April).

———. 1970. "Trade Credit and the Money Market," *Journal of Political Economy* Vol. 78, No.2 (March/April).

Wojnilower, Albert M. 1980. "The Central Role of Credit Crunches in Recent Financial History," *Brookings Papers on Economic Activity 2*. Brookings Institution, Washington, DC.

5

Inflation, Money, and Stock Prices:
An Alternative Interpretation
Victor A. Canto, M.C. Findlay,
and Marc R. Reinganum

SUMMARY

Over the last two decades, the finance and economics literature has contained substantial research on the relation between money and inflation and stock prices, while monetary economics has remained devoted to the study of the relation of money and inflation. Little effort has been made to integrate the two.

Empirical studies do not support the conventional contention that a positive association between changes in the money supply and stock returns would imply a positive association between inflation and stock returns. A simple empirical text finds a negative relation between inflation and changes in money (M1) based on monthly data from February 1961 through December 1983.

To maintain a monetary view of inflation, there must be a relevant monetary aggregate that is determined exogenously. If money is endogenous, then by definition money cannot cause inflation. The negative correlation between higher monetary aggregates and inflation can be viewed as the result of the optimal behavior of economic agents as they adjust their money holdings.

Several specific predictions, which are consistent with the above findings, are suggested by this explanation:

This essay has appeared previously as V.A. Canto, M.C. Findlay, and Marc R. Reinganum, "Inflation, Money and Stock Prices: An Alternative Interpretation," *The Financial Review* February 1985, Vol.20, No.1, pp.95–105. Reprinted with permission.

- Inflation causes changes in M1. To minimize the inflation tax, economic agents will substitute out of M1 into interest-bearing assets. This substitution will induce a negative correlation between M1 and inflation.
- Changes in the monetary base cause inflation. Therefore, changes. in the monetary base will be positively correlated with inflation.
- Changes in stock returns will lead to changes in M1. Increases in expected future activity would increase current stock returns and subsequently the demand for M1, as in the Fama (1981) and Nelson (1979) arguments. However, with M1 endogenous, a change in its demand will induce a change in its supply. Hence, a positive but spurious correlation between changes in M1 and stock returns will be observed.

INFLATION AND CHANGES IN "MONEY"

Over the last two decades, the finance and economics literature has contained substantial research on the relation between money and stock prices and the relation between inflation and stock prices. Monetary economics, of course, has been concerned with the much older inquiry into the relation between money and inflation. Until recently, surprisingly little effort has been devoted to integrating the results of these various lines of research. The purposes of this essay are (1) to expose an apparent inconsistency in the findings of earlier research and (2) to offer an alternative interpretation of these results to that found in more recent research.

The literature on money and stock prices has been surveyed recently by Sorensen (1982). In his and other papers (Rozeff 1974; Rogalski and Vinso 1977), a positive association between changes in the money supply and stock returns is reported. With Sorensen's methodology, an increase in unanticipated money (for example, M1B) growth is associated with an increase in the level of the Standard & Poor's 500 stock market index. The positive association is found both contemporaneously and with the stock market leading money by one and two quarters. The results, however, are consistent with market efficiency.

Given a strong prior belief that changes in the money supply cause inflation, one might reason that a positive association between changes in the money supply and stock returns would imply a positive associa-

We wish to thank Fischer Black, Doug Joines, and Truman Clark for their helpful comments.

tion between inflation and stock returns. Although the conventional wisdom indicated that stocks were an inflation hedge, such reasoning is not supported by empirical work. In perhaps the most well-known study of stock returns and inflation, Fama and Schwert (1977) report:

> Common stock returns are negatively related to the expected inflation rate during the 1953–1971 period. Although the results are less consistent, common stock returns also seem to be negatively related to the unexpected inflation rate and to changes in the expected inflation rate. Thus, contrary to long-held beliefs, but in line with accumulating empirical evidence, common stocks are rather perverse as hedges against inflation. (p. 144)

Jointly, these results suggest a basic anomaly. Consider the following simple regressions:

$$R_n = \alpha_0 + \alpha_1 \pi + \epsilon \tag{1}$$

$$R_n = \beta_0 + \beta_1 M + \mu \tag{2}$$

$$\pi = \gamma_0 + \gamma_1 M + \xi, \tag{3}$$

where

R_n = nominal stock returns
π = inflation rate
M = Growth rate of the money supply.

Substituting π from Equation 3 into Equation 1, one obtains

$$R_n = (\alpha_0 + \alpha_1 \gamma_0 + \alpha_1 \xi) + (\alpha_1 \gamma_1) M + \epsilon. \tag{4}$$

A comparison of Equations 2 and 4 reveals that $\beta_1 = \alpha_1 \gamma_1$. While the money and stock returns literature suggests that $\beta_1 > 0$, the inflation and stock returns literature suggests that $\alpha_1 < 0$. Assuming this simple structure, these results are consistent only if $\gamma_1 < 0$. Stated differently, the earlier empirical work suggests that inflation and changes in the money supply are *negatively* correlated.

It might thus appear that the generally accepted view of a positive relation between money and inflation is contradicted. Of course, one might argue that the variables are interrelated in a more complex way, or that the earlier empirical results are sample specific. However, a simple empirical test finds a negative relation between inflation and changes in money (M1) based on monthly data from February 1961 through December 1983.[1] In Table 5.1, contemporaneous and 12 lagged values of the seasonal differences in the growth rate of M1 are regressed on seasonal differences in the inflation rate. The results indicate a significant negative contemporaneous relation. The lagged values, taken together, are not significantly different from zero. Although not reported, the regression was run over the 1961–71 and 1972–83 subperiods with findings similar to those reported in Table 5.1. Thus, the negative relation between inflation and changes in the money supply implied by these two literatures has been observed for more than two decades.

TABLE 5.1. Contemporaneous and 12 Lagged Values of the Seasonal Differences in the Growth Rate of M1 (Not Seasonally Adjusted) Regressed on Seasonal Differences in the Consumer Price Index (Not Seasonally Adjusted), Monthly Data, February 1961 through December 1983

Independent Variable	Parameter Estimate	Standard Error
Intercept	7.2×10^{-5}	2.1×10^{-4}
$\Delta M1_t$	-0.1087	0.0379
$\Delta M1_{t-1}$	-0.0007	0.0347
$\Delta M1_{t-2}$	-0.0454	0.0352
$\Delta M1_{t-3}$	0.0156	0.0347
$\Delta M1_{t-4}$	0.0334	0.0345
$\Delta M1_{t-5}$	0.0292	0.0346
$\Delta M1_{t-6}$	0.0364	0.0344
$\Delta M1_{t-7}$	-0.0450	0.0346
$\Delta M1_{t-8}$	-0.0124	0.0349
$\Delta M1_{t-9}$	0.0385	0.0350
$\Delta M1_{t-10}$	0.0159	0.0357
$\Delta M1_{t-11}$	0.0272	0.0362
$\Delta M1_{t-12}$	-0.0653	0.0399
Sum of lags	0.0272	0.1115

Note: $\Delta M1_t = (1 - B)(1 - B^{12}) \ln M1_t$, where B is the Box–Jenkins backshift operator. The dependent variable is $(1 - B)(1 - B^{12}) \ln$ consumer price index.

INFLATION AND CHANGES IN MONETARY STOCK

As explained above, the money/stock return and the inflation/stock return literatures, taken together, imply a negative correlation between changes in the money supply and inflation. While this negative relation is observed empirically, it would seem to be at variance with the long-held monetary view of inflation.

A simple explanation that might resolve these conflicts is that money, at least as measured in the above studies, is endogenous. This view of money is not new and has been espoused by authors such as Black (1972). Naturally, if money is endogenous, then by definition money cannot cause inflation. To maintain a monetary view of inflation, there must be a relevant monetary aggregate that is determined exogenously. In principle, the monetary base is under the control of government authorities and can be assumed to be exogenous.

In Table 5.2, contemporaneous and 12 lagged values of the seasonal differences in growth rate of the monetary base [that is, $(1-B)(1-B^{12})$ 1n base] are regressed on seasonal differences in the inflation rate. Using monthly data from February 1961 through December 1983, the contemporaneous relation is positive but within two standard errors of zero. However, all lagged values taken together indicate a positive and statistically significant relation; 10 of the 12 lagged coefficients are positive. Overall, the relation is positive and significant. These results were also found in the 1972–83 subperiod, although no significant relations were detected in the 1961–71 subperiod.[2] Thus, these empirical results are consistent with the monetary view of inflation when money is narrowly defined as the monetary base, at least since 1972.

Why is the relation between higher monetary aggregates and inflation negative? Suppose one is focusing on M1, which is non-interest bearing. Standard price theory would suggest that an increase in expected inflation would induce a shift toward interest-bearing assets and out of M1.[3] Hence, M1 becomes endogenous. Changes in the monetary base cause inflation, and economic agents adjust their monetary holdings in response to the inflation. Thus, the negative correlation between these two variables can be viewed as the result of the optimal behavior of economic agents as they adjust their monetary holdings.

In this essay a simple Box–Jenkins Autoregressive Integrated Moving Average (ARIMA) model is used to separate inflation and money growth into their anticipated and unanticipated components. This is a mechanical way to separate the anticipated and unanticipated components,

TABLE 5.2. Contemporaneous and 12 Lagged Values of the Seasonal Differences in the Growth Rate of the Monetary Base (Not Seasonally Adjusted) Regressed on Seasonal Differences in the Consumer Price Index (Not Seasonally Adjusted), Monthly Data, February 1961 through December 1983

Independent Variable	Parameter Estimate	Standard Error
Intercept	1.1×10^{-5}	2.1×10^{-4}
ΔBase_t	0.0106	0.0134
ΔBase_{t-1}	0.0177	0.0152
ΔBase_{t-2}	-0.0022	0.0161
ΔBase_{t-3}	0.0214	0.0159
ΔBase_{t-4}	0.0290	0.0159
ΔBase_{t-5}	0.0417	0.0159
ΔBase_{t-6}	0.0143	0.0158
ΔBase_{t-7}	0.0099	0.0159
ΔBase_{t-8}	0.0122	0.0159
ΔBase_{t-9}	0.0160	0.0159
$\Delta \text{Base}_{t-10}$	0.0218	0.0160
$\Delta \text{Base}_{t-11}$	0.0244	0.0152
$\Delta \text{Base}_{t-12}$	-0.0030	0.0134
Sum of lags	0.2031	0.0913

Note: $\Delta \text{Base}_t = (1 - B)(1 - B^{12}) \ln \text{Base}_t$, where B is the Box–Jenkins backshift operator. The dependent variable is $(1 - B)(1 - B^{12}) \ln$ consumer price index.

and it may not yield the "true" unanticipated component. Alternative mechanical rules could be used to extract the unanticipated component. However, empirical research in the money and stock return literature suggests that the results are not sensitive to the mechanical rules used [contrast Rogalski and Vinso (1977) with Sorensen (1982)].

A MORE SPECIFIC AND OPERATIONAL MONETARIST VIEW OF INFLATION

Recent research suggests more complicated ways by which the monetary view of inflation might be sustained. For example, Nelson (1979) and Fama (1981) allow for changes in the demand for money. A change in expected real economic activity will be associated with changes in money demand and stock returns in the same direction, as long as the stock market is a leading indicator of real economic activity. If the exogenously determined money supply is held constant, inflation should move in the opposite direction to money demand. Hence, a negative, but spurious, correlation between stock returns and inflation would be observed because of an intervening shift in money demand. Of course, by allowing for money demand shifts, any observed relation between money supply and inflation can be explained.

In contrast, the resolution of the apparent contradictory findings proposed here focuses on a single source of demand shifts. In particular, demand shifts are assumed to occur as economic agents shift wealth between interest and non-interest-bearing deposits. Several specific predictions, which are consistent with the above findings, are suggested by this explanation:

First, inflation causes changes in M1. To minimize the inflation tax, economic agents will substitute out of M1 into interest-bearing assets. This substitution will induce a negative correlation between M1 and inflation.

Second, changes in the monetary base cause inflation. Therefore, changes in the monetary base will be positively correlated with inflation.

Third, changes in stock returns will lead changes in M1. Increases in expected future activity would increase current stock returns and subsequently the demand for M1, as in the Fama (1981) and Nelson (1979) arguments. However, with M1 endogenous, a change in its demand will induce a change in its supply. Hence, a positive but spurious correlation between changes in M1 and stock returns will be observed.

In conclusion, the empirical complications with the monetary view of inflation could be resolved simply if one very narrowly defined money as the monetary base and permitted higher monetary aggregates to be determined endogenously in the economic system. That is, changes in the growth rate of the monetary base will result in a higher inflation rate, all else the same. This analysis still leaves unexplained the observed negative relation between stock returns and inflation. We suspect that this negative relation requires a nonmonetary explanation. For example, shocks in the real sector of the economy may affect stock returns and the price level in opposite directions. Naturally, further empirical research is necessary to corroborate these predictions.

NOTES

1. A consistently defined M1 time series from January 1959 through December 1983 has been made available recently by the Federal Reserve and is used here. Because of the definition of the variables and the structure of the regressions, the first observation with complete data for all the independent variables is February 1961.

2. Gordon (1982) argued that the money supply process changed in 1967, which coincided with the beginning of the disintegration of the Bretton Woods system.

3. We recognize that banks may be able to pay implicit interest rates on checking account balances in a variety of ways. However, to the extent that currency is non-interest bearing, and the implicit interest payment is below market rates, the substitution effect between M1 and other interest-bearing assets still will result.

REFERENCES

Black, Fischer. 1972. "Active and Passive Money in a Neoclassical Model." *Journal of Finance,* 27, pp. 801–14 (September).

Fama, Eugene F. 1981. "Stock Returns, Real Activity, Inflation and Money." *American Economic Review,* 71, pp. 545–65 (September).

Fama, Eugene F., and G. William Schwert. 1977. "Asset Returns and Inflation." *Journal of Financial Economics,* 5, pp. 113–46.

Gordon, Robert J. 1982. "Price Inertia and Policy Ineffectiveness in the United States, 1890–1980." *Journal of Political Economy,* 90, pp. 1087–1117 (December).

Nelson, Charles. 1979. "Recursive Structure in U.S. Income, Prices, and Output." *Journal of Political Economy,* 87, pp.1307–27 (December).

Rogalski, Richard, and Joseph Vinso. 1977. "Stock Returns, Money Supply and the Direction of Causality." *Journal of Finance,* 32, pp. 1017–30 (September).

Rozeff, Michael. 1974. "Money and Stock Prices." *Journal of Financial Economics,* 1, pp. 245–302 (September).

Sorensen, Eric. 1982. "Rational Expectations and the Impact of Money upon Stock Prices." *Journal of Financial and Quantitative Analysis,* 17, pp. 649–62 (December).

6

Reinstatement of the Dollar: The Blueprint
Arthur B. Laffer

SUMMARY

The issue of a gold-based monetary system has again come of age. The impulse originates in the debacle of the current system in which inflation and rising interest rates have reached epidemic proportions. The threat of monetary disintegration provides fertile ground for a radical change in the world's monetary system; an early reinstatement of the dollar as a world currency convertible into gold no longer is inconceivable. The pressing issue is whether a return to a gold standard will be used to avert a financial collapse or come in its aftermath.

Restoration of a link between gold and the dollar does not per se guarantee stability. Done improperly, such a policy change could cause enormous dislocations to the economy. The blueprint for a successful return to dollar convertibility, presented here, includes a transition period to ensure that it is the gold market, not the economy, that makes the initial adjustment inherent in a return to a gold-based monetary system. "Safety valves" also are provided to minimize the chances of altercations in the gold market being forced upon the economy as a whole.

This essay makes extensive use of Federal Reserve Chairman Paul Volcker's ideas as found in the 1972 U.S. proposals to the International Monetary Fund (*Economic Report of the President* 1973). By virtue of his position, Volcker is key to reinstatement of the dollar. Implementation of such a policy change would spur growth in real output, personal income, and corporate profits. Stockmarkets throughout the world would rise and interest rates fall in recognition of the benefits that would accrue to the global economy and political order from the United States reaffirming its responsibility to provide a stable, world numeraire.

THE FAILURE OF THE UNHINGED MONETARY SYSTEM

The experiment with an unhinged monetary system has by any measure been a debacle. The break between the dollar and gold was undertaken in the name of prosperity, high employment, and economic stability. The monetary authorities, relieved of the "artificial discipline" to exchange liabilities of the central bank into some barbaric metal at a fixed rate, would be free to pursue full employment policies even if they required some short-run increases in inflation. The accompanying devaluation of the dollar against gold and most foreign currencies, it was promised, would restore the competitiveness of the U.S. economy. Cheaper currency would win markets back for U.S. producers and restore jobs for U.S. workers. The trade account, which had been deteriorating, would improve.

A brief revisitation of the economic events surrounding the full demonetization of gold and the unhinging of the dollar, however, illustrates the extent to which the new monetary system failed to deliver on its promises. The U.S. withdrawal from the gold pool and the elimination of private dollar convertibility into gold occurred in March 1968. The establishment of a fully inconvertible dollar began on August 15, 1971. While these two dates present a false sense of precision, they are nonetheless good points of demarcation for what was actually an emerging process. When juxtaposed against the previous period, the calendar years following these dates offer a starkly vivid picture of the decline of the U.S. economy. In 1967 the official price of gold was $35 per ounce, and it traded at that price in private markets. By 1970 that price had risen to $47 and in January 1980 gold briefly hit its all-time high of $875. For all of 1980 the price of gold averaged more than $600 per ounce. This rise reflects a more than 17-fold increase in some 13 years.

Other economic indicators display similar patterns. Inflation as measured by the consumer price index rose from a 3 percent annual rate in 1967 to a 5.5 percent rate in 1970 and then surged to the 13.3 percent rate experienced in 1979. The pattern of three-month Treasury bill rates parallels the inflation movements remarkably well. In 1967 these three-month bill rates averaged 4.3 percent. By 1970 they averaged 6.5 percent. A decade later they averaged 11.5 percent. In 1981 they peaked at an average rate of 14 percent.

In tandem, the dollar fell in value when measured in terms of German marks, Swiss francs, and several other currencies. In 1967 four marks exchanged for one dollar, as did 4.3 Swiss francs. By 1970 the ratio had become 3.6 marks and still 4.3 Swiss francs. During the third quarter of 1980, the full extent of the dollar collapse could be seen in that dollars could then be purchased at a price of only 1.75 marks and 1.63 Swiss francs.

The real side of the economy suffered as well during the monetary collapse. The rate of unemployment stood at 3.8 percent in 1967. It rose to 4.9 percent in 1970 and 7.1 percent in 1980, peaking at 10.7 percent at the end of 1982. As recently as 1982, the Dow Jones industrial average was below its 1967 level. When measured in units of constant purchasing power, the decline has been extraordinary. Even the federal deficit has become engorged over these years. In 1967 the red ink totaled $8.7 billion, in 1970 it was $2.8 billion, in 1980 it was $59.6 billion, and in 1983 it stood at $195.4 billion.

THE RETURN TO A GOLD STANDARD

It is hardly surprising that, whatever its merits, the monetary system is being barraged with heated assaults. Since 1982 much progress has been made toward returning to a formal price rule. The monetary authorities' maniacal allegiance to targeting the quantity of money has given way to a more eclectic, all-indicators approach that allows for stabilization of commodity prices and interest rates. An early return to a gold standard is no longer inconceivable. In my view, the probabilities that the United States will return to a convertible dollar have become high enough to justify describing the likely shape and implications of a specific program to restore dollar convertibility.

A return to a gold standard should not be embraced impulsively or implemented by surprise. Done improperly, dollar convertibility could cause egregious dislocations to the financial markets and the economy. If the price of gold were to be set too high, for example, inflation would continue to rise. Interest rates would reach new highs. If, on the other hand, the price of gold were set too low, the price level would fall, leading to deflationary pressures throughout the economy. Moreover, if the technical aspects of the program were defective, announcement of a return to dollar convertibility could create a speculative run on U.S. gold reserves that would abort the attempt to restore gold backing to the dollar.

A properly designed program should have as its initial goal the stabilization of prices generally at or near their current level. Second, the program must be credible and workable. Finally, it should be designed to protect the general economy from shocks to the gold market per se, disturbances that have nothing to do with monetary policy. Stated simply, a workable system of gold/dollar convertibility must not permit the economy to experience wrenching adjustments because of changes in gold. If shocks to the gold market do occur, any responsible system must permit the price of gold to do the adjusting. Therefore, safety valves must be included.

As chairman of the Board of Governors of the Federal Reserve System, and as one of the preeminently successful and influential central bankers of our time, Paul Volcker will have substantial influence over any reform of the U.S. or international monetary system. Any radical change in U.S. monetary order therefore presumably would require not only Volcker's acquiescence, but more likely his enthusiastic support even if he resigns as chairman of the Fed. Based upon his posturing since the late 1960s, it is, in my opinion, quite conceivable that Volcker could actually lead the search for a new order. While undersecretary of the Treasury during the hectic monetary gyrations of the early 1970s, Volcker was reported to be the last to abandon the need for maintaining the dollar's convertibility into gold. In fact, it was rumored that even after the enormous dollar devaluations, Volcker expected and argued in favor of a return to convertibility.

Volcker is, in my view, the most knowledgeable high-ranking bureaucrat on monetary affairs in the United States. His history at the U.S. Treasury goes back to 1951 and covers positions such as undersecretary of the Treasury, president of the New York Fed, and now chairman of the Board of Governors of the Federal Reserve System. He has been one of the singlemost involved operatives in each of these positions. Moreover, Volcker singlehandedly carried out the negotiations with the international community throughout the entire monetary reordering of the world in the 1970s. Of quite some importance is the fact that the design of "The U.S. Proposals for Using Reserves As an Indicator of the Need for Balance-of-Payments Adjustment" (*Economic Report of the President* 1973) presented at the Nairobi International Monetary Fund meetings in 1972 was attributed to him. As principal U.S. representative to these meetings, then-Treasury Secretary George P. Shultz formally presented the proposal.

The Blueprint

Given my perception of the situations, one could well imagine a re-ordering of the world's monetary system and the reemergence of gold convertibility in something of the following form:

The United States would announce a double-faceted program providing for the restoration of dollar convertibility into gold. The first part of the program would allow a transition period designed to permit the gold market in particular, and financial markets in general, to adjust to dollar convertibility before its implementation. The need for such a period was widely recognized in 1972. "The U.S. Proposals" stated:

> We merely want to note that some generally acceptable transitional arrangements are necessary. This transitional problem is not unique to the proposed system. Any monetary system based upon concepts of equilibrium and convertibility will require special measures to deal with transitional problems. (*Economic Report of the President* 1973, p. 171)

The second part of the program would provide the requisite technical specifications necessary to make the new monetary system workable and credible. As in 1972 the proposal outlined below visualizes

> a system in which disproportionately large gains in reserves for a particular country indicate the need for adjustment measures to eliminate a balance-of-payments surplus, just as, in any system of convertibility into reserve assets, disproportionately large losses of reserves indicate the need for adjustment to eliminate a balance-of-payments deficit. (p. 160)

The transition phase would encompass the following policy initiatives:

- The United States would announce its full intention of returning to a convertible dollar at some prespecified time in the future, say, three months.
- At the time of this pre-gold-price-fixing announcement, the United States also would provide the financial markets with as much potentially relevant information as could be made available. Gold and other metal stockpiles would be enumerated precisely. This would require a resurrection of the Treasury's gold budget, which was abandoned in the early 1970s.
- The United States could announce during this three-month interval, neither the Federal Reserve nor the U.S. Treasury would in-

tervene in the foreign exchange markets or have any net intervention in the open market. Net loans of reserves to member banks in the Federal Reserve System through the discount window would also be frozen at their current level. Stated simply, during this three-month interval, the Federal Reserve and Treasury would "take a vacation" so as not to disrupt the natural forces in the private market. The monetary base would, as a result of the absence of actions, remain literally unchanged during this interval.

The same announcement would outline the actual exchange mechanism linking the dollar to gold. It would read something like this:

- Three months hence, the Federal Reserve has been instructed to establish parity between dollar unit of its liabilities (currency in circulation and member bank reserves) and a fixed quantity of gold at that day's average transaction price in the London gold market. This will be the official value of the dollar and intervention price of gold. During the next month:
  - The Federal Reserve will stand ready to sell a total of 1 million ounces of gold to all demanders at a price 0.7 percent higher than the official price in exchange for units of its liabilities (monetary base).
  - The Federal Reserve will stand ready to purchase a total of 1 million ounces of gold from all sellers at a price of 0.7 percent below its official price in exchange for units of its liabilities.
  - If more than 1 million ounces of gold is purchased net from the Fed or offered net to the Fed, intervention will cease and the dollar price of gold will be allowed to change.
- Thirty days after the initial intervention date, the Federal Reserve will commit to buy or sell a total of 2 million ounces of gold at the respective intervention points.
- If the parity established on the initial intervention date has not been broken, the intervention points will remain unchanged.
- If the parity established on the initial intervention date has been broken, then a new parity between the dollar and gold will be established at that day's average transaction price in the London gold market.
- Sixty days after the initial intervention date, and every 30 days thereafter, the amount of gold the Federal Reserve will commit to

buy or sell will double until the value of committed gold reserves exceeds 10 percent of the dollar value of the Federal Reserve's liabilities. If at any point the net amount of gold bought or sold exceeds the amount of gold committed, dollar/gold parity will be broken and intervention will cease. The dollar price of gold once again will be reset in the marketplace and parity reestablished at the beginning of the next 30-day period.

- Once the value of committed gold reserves exceeds 10 percent of the dollar value of the Federal Reserve's liabilities, the then-prevailing parity will be considered the official price of gold.
- When valued at the official price, the Federal Reserve will attempt over time to establish an average dollar value of gold reserves equal to 40 percent of the dollar value of its liabilities. This average reserve will be a "target reserve quantity" around which policy operates.
- A gold reserve band will be instituted whereby a reserve level equal to 70 percent of the dollar value of the Federal Reserve's liabilities will be designated as the upper reserve limit and a reserve level equal to 10 percent of its liabilities will be designated as the lower reserve limit.
- Once established, the target reserve quantity of gold will determine the mandatory policy trigger points. Within a band of 25 percent on either side of the target reserve level, the monetary authorities will have full discretion in exercising control over the monetary base. As long as the monetary authority maintains the official price via direct convertibility, there will be no strictures placed on actions taken to change the monetary base. Open market operations, discounting, and even exchange rate interventions will be solely under the discretion of the monetary authority as long as the dollar value of the quantity of gold is between 0.30 and 0.50 of the monetary base, that is, within the 25 percent band of target reserves.
- If actual reserves were, however, to fall within the range of 0.20 to 0.30 of the monetary base, then the monetary authority's discretion will be removed in its entirety. The monetary authority will be required to run policies such that the monetary base will experience absolutely no growth. This, in effect, means that the monetary authority will be required to offset fully any gold/dollar conversion as long as actual gold reserves fall between one-half and three-quarters of the target reserve level (0.20 and 0.30 of the monetary base).

- If, in spite of the cessation of the growth of the monetary base, actual reserves fall by between 50 and 25 percent of target reserves (0.10 and 0.20 of the monetary base), the monetary authority will then be compelled to contract the monetary base at the rate of 1 percent per month. This means that the monetary authority must act to effectuate a decline in the monetary base of 1 percent per month, inclusive of the monetary base effects of maintaining gold convertibility. If the decline in the base due solely to gold sales is greater than, or less than, 1 percent, then open market operations will be used to limit or increase, respectively, the change in the base to the prescribed amount.
- A symmetric set of mandatory policy dicta result when actual reserves grow to between 1.25 and 1.5 of target reserves and 1.5 and 1.75 of target reserves. The monetary base rules in each of these ranges are an increase of 1 and 2 percent per month, respectively, again inclusive of all gold/dollar conversions.
- If the gold reserve protection measures fail to preserve the actual value of reserves between 0.25 and 1.75 of the target level of reserves while maintaining convertibility, all gold/dollar conversion provisions cease. The dollar's convertibility will be temporarily suspended, and the dollar price of gold will be set free for a three-month adjustment period.
- During this temporary period of inconvertibility, the monetary authorities will be required to suspend all actions that would affect the monetary base. Again, the price of gold will be reset as before and convertibility will be reinstated.

Once the official price for gold is established, the actual reserves of gold held by the monetary authority will be different from the level of target reserves. If, as appears most likely for an initial move back to convertibility, the actual amount of reserves is in excess of the amounts needed for the target reserves, then this gold should be segregated and sold in a systematic manner. A reasonable solution would be to sell the entire amount in equal monthly installments over a five-year period. Quite symmetrically, if there were a deficiency, there should be a five-year plan to acquire gold in equal monthly amounts. The deficiency or surplus should have no bearing on the monetary authority's behavior. In the monetary authority's account for the purposes of maintaining dollar convertibility, the initial amount of gold would be the target reserve quantity, or 40 percent of the monetary base.

With the value of the dollar defined in terms of gold, there would no longer exist any reason for the U.S. government to be concerned with the foreign exchange value of the dollar. The official policy of the United States should remain that the dollar would be free to seek its own level on foreign exchange markets. The United States should concern itself neither with foreign official intervention nor with the fluctuations in foreign exchange rates. It is quite likely that many foreign governments would be quick to reestablish parity between their currencies and the dollar. With the dollar as good as gold, the attraction would be great.

Links to "The U.S. Proposals" of 1972

The approach outlined above includes several key concepts put forward in "The U.S. Proposals" of 1972 (*Economic Report of the President* 1973). First, the need for a "base" level of reserves, the "target reserve quantity," was recognized. Forty percent was selected as the illustrative amount in the above proposal because it approximates the pre-1934 relationship between gold reserves and the monetary base in the United States within the Federal Reserve Bank System (Krooss and Samuelson 1969).

Second, as the text of "The U.S. Proposals" reveals, changes in the level of gold or primary reserves are used as the key policy variable:

> Reserves are more comprehensive, more reliable and more quickly available indicators than other criteria of external balance. While reserves may be distorted in the short-run, no other single series provides a superior basis for analysis. In a convertibility system, reserve data are necessarily indicative of disequilibrium in the adjustment process; this has always been understood in terms of inducements to adjust for deficit countries—and the concept applies with equal logic to adjustment needs for surplus countries. (p. 173)

The use of reserve bands also was part of the 1972 proposal and no doubt incorporates much of Volcker's technical inputs. "Under a reserve-indicator system," says "The U.S. Proposals," "certain points would be established above and below each country's base level to guide the adjustment process and to assure even-handed convertibility disciplines" (p. 166). A "low point," "lower warning point," and "outer point" are recommended as trigger mechanisms for appropriate policy responses to restore equilibrium.

> Countries would not be expected to ignore imbalances blithely until their disequilibria had become so extreme as to prompt strong international concern

through the indicator mechanism. Reserve fluctuations would signal emerging disequilibria; movement to outer indicators signalling strong international concern would occur only when countries failed to make the appropriate responses as the disequilibria built up. (p. 164)

Later, the proposal states:

The purpose of a reserve-indicator system is to provide strong incentives for countries to act in limited steps, using a variety of tools suited to their circumstances before their situation becomes so urgent as to involve international concern and action. (p. 169)

PROBLEMS AND SOLUTIONS

The above proposal would attempt to rectify two serious defects inherent in most systems to return to gold convertibility. The original fixing price of gold no longer would be left to the vicissitudes of political pressures. With full knowledge, the market and its transactors, with the threat of losses and the hopes of profit, would select the appropriate price for gold. This would thus avoid the necessity of making the overall economy adjust to some inappropriate price of gold.

As was pointed out in this 1972 U.S. monetary proposal:

A decision to provide the system with too few reserves induces—and sanctions—a destabilizing and ultimately fruitless competition for scarce reserves. Creation of too many reserves pushes too great a share of the adjustment pressure onto surplus countries and facilitates world inflation. (p. 164)

Allowing the price of gold to adjust would minimize this problem by permitting gold's original price setting to accommodate the economy, instead of forcing the economy to adjust to a price set by government fiat.

The second criticism to which this proposal is responsive is an explicit change in the market for gold itself. If gold became excessively plentiful or scarce owing to conditions beyond the control of the monetary authority, it would make no sense whatsoever to force the economy to either deflate or inflate to accommodate an altered market for gold itself. Whenever such disturbances occurred, the dollar would be defended until excessive reserves of gold were acquired or lost. At such a time, the price of gold would again be set free and allowed to adjust to the overall economy.

Another issue that invariably arises when discussing gold convertibility is the role to be played by gold coins. As a matter of practice, the
issue is neither complex nor central to the workings of an effective system. Nonetheless, if coins are to circulate and be used as money, the value
of the coin when used as money must be greater than the value of the metal
contained in the coin. If the value of the metal were equal to or greater
than the monetary value, coins would be melted down and would disap-
pear from circulation. The value of the coin as a money need not be much
in excess of the value of the metal. In fact, gold coins today have a
premium of less than 10 percent unless they have other characteristics.
It would seem reasonable, then, that the monetary authority would mint
gold coins and place them in circulation. Counterfeiting legislation should
also be enacted to guarantee the quality of circulating coins. The mint-
ing of gold coins is a natural way for the monetary authority to rid itself
of gold reserves in excess of those to be held against the monetary base.

IMPLICATIONS

A policy change leading back to dollar convertibility along these lines
would change dramatically the outlook for inflation, the economy, and
harmony among the industrial nations.

The inflationary expectations still evident in U.S. financial markets
would fall precipitously. With the monetary system hinged to the real
world through gold—a surrogate for all goods and services—price stability
and certainty about the future would return in short order. Announcement
of the program alone would tend to increase confidence in the dollar, leading to an incipient excess demand for dollars relative to their supply. This
is a necessary condition to arresting inflation. The growth in the monetary aggregates would tend to accelerate to accommodate this excess demand for dollars. Velocity would fall such that this increase in money
would be consistent with lower rates of inflation (Kadlec and Laffer 1979).
For example, if the velocity of money measured by nominal gross national
product divided by M1 were to decline to its 1967 level of 4.45, the money
supply at today's level of real output could expand by more than 50 percent with no change in the price level.

Interest rates over horizons both near and far would fall. Most likely,
the greatest initial adjustment would be in short-term maturities. As confidence extended out over longer time horizons, longer-term rates would
continue to decline. The more credible the program, the more precipitous the decline in interest rates (Kadlec and Laffer 1979).

Once the dollar were as good as gold, demand for dollars would surge in international markets as well. The foreign exchange value of the dollar would tend to rise. Foreign monetary authorities, however, might offset this shift in demand out of their own currencies into the dollar through offsetting foreign exchange operations, that is, selling dollar reserve assets into the foreign exchange markets in exchange for their domestic money. Such a move by foreign monetary authorities would be all to the good. By securing the value of their currencies relative to the dollar, their monetary systems, too, would be linked through the dollar to gold. Inflationary expectations and interest rates would fall in these currencies as well (Kadlec and Laffer 1979).

Benefits also would accrue to the real sector of the economy. Uncertainty over the value of money in terms of both goods and the cost of financing is itself an impediment to capital formation. It is an additional external factor outside of the control of management that increases the risk of engaging in long-term investment.

Moreover, the sharp reduction in the rate of inflation that would ensue with a return to dollar convertibility would diminish the illusory component of corporate profits due to undercosting of goods sold and under-depreciation of fixed assets. Effective tax rates on corporate profits would fall. Real after-tax returns would rise. Corporate economic activity and profits would expand (Laffer and Ranson 1979).

The stock market would rise. Two factors would be evident: First, expected future after-tax profits would be higher, because of the expansion in corporate activity and the reduction in effective tax rates. Second, the real value of these profits would more closely approximate reported profits—smaller adjustments would have to be made to correct for illusory gains. Thus, price/earnings ratios based on accounting profits would go up.

Individuals would benefit by a return to dollar convertibility for similar reasons. Resources devoted to protecting savings from the danger of unexpected changes in the value of the dollar in terms of goods, for example, purchasing gold coins, foreign exchange, etc., would be directed toward increasing production and wealth. "Bracket creep"—the rise of nominal incomes into higher tax brackets even while real incomes remain constant—also would cease, removing the expectation of ever-increasing effective personal income tax rates without legislative relief (Laffer and Ranson 1979). Employment would rise, unemployment would fall.

The financial health of the government also would improve. The interest expense of the federal deficit for fiscal year 1984 was $154 billion—the third largest budget item. A fall in interest rates per se would reduce the cost of financing the government debt. The expansion in the economy following a restoration of dollar convertibility also would increase the tax base—leading to an increase in revenues. In a healthy economic environment, demands for government spending decline. Higher tax revenues and lower spending directly reduce the deficit.

Finally, the return to dollar convertibility would reinstate the United States as central banker to the world. The importance of this change is difficult to underestimate. For almost a decade, the world has been without a numeraire, a North Star by which to guide international commerce and investment. The resulting cumulative economic inefficiencies have subtracted from the wealth of all nations. It is not too much to say that many of the political and social tensions of the era have been due in part to these real costs. With the dollar once again the world numeraire, these inefficiencies would be removed, and global resources freed would be employed toward productive ends.

New York's position as the center of world finance would be elevated and the competitive position of U.S. banks would be enhanced relative to London and other overseas money centers. But all Western commercial centers would gain in the absolute expansion of global wealth. Assuming most of the major trading nations of the world would link their currencies to the dollar, global inflation would be effectively arrested. Inflation's destructive impact on domestic economies would be curbed as well, although the need for global tax reforms would remain to offset the effects of a dozen years of inflation on fiscal systems.

Transcending these not inconsequential commercial considerations, though, are the benefits that restoration of the dollar as a stable world currency would bring to world political order. Protectionist pressures in the West would be mitigated, although not eliminated. An element of cohesion would be returned to the Western alliance, which along with the present monetary system threatens fracture and disintegration.

Throughout history, it has been the world's premier economic and military power that has put its strength and responsibility behind the maintenance of a stable world currency. The United States abandoned this element of global leadership when it unhinged the dollar from gold. It is not within the capacity of any other nation or cluster of nations to take on this responsibility. The United States can signal its willingness to resume this critical role by once again placing the dollar within the disciplined framework outlined here.

REFERENCES

Economic Report of the President. 1973. "The U.S. Proposals for Using Reserves As an Indicator of the Need for Balance-of-Payments Adjustment," Supplement to Chapter 5. Government Printing Office, Washington, DC (January), pp. 160–74.

Kadlec, Charles W., and Laffer, Arthur B. 1979. "The Monetary Crisis: A Classical Perspective." *Economic Study,* A.B. Laffer Associates, Lomita, CA (November 12).

Krooss, Herman E., and Samuelson, Paul A. 1969. *Documentary History of Banking and Currency in the United States.* New York: McGraw-Hill, p. 2457.

Laffer, Arthur B., and Ranson, David R. 1979. "Inflation, Taxes and Equity Values." *Economic Study,* H. C. Wainwright & Co. Economics, Boston (September 20).

7

Trade Policy and the U.S. Economy
Victor A. Canto, Arthur B. Laffer, and James C. Turney

SUMMARY

After a decade of slow economic growth and rising unemployment, nations are seeking ways to improve their trade balances in order to promote domestic prosperity. But protectionist policies—currency devaluations, import tariffs, export subsidies, and quotas—do not work. Indeed, they frequently harm the economies and trade positions of those countries using them.

Currency devaluations are as often as not associated with above-average inflation in the devaluing country and a deterioration in the trade account in the years following the devaluation. Nor do tariffs and quotas improve the trade balance; although they reduce the level of imports, they also reduce the level of exports, leaving the net trade balance unchanged. Conversely, export subsidies increase both exports and imports, leaving the net result unchanged.

The concern over improving the trade balance as a condition for a healthy economy and rising employment is misplaced. More often than not, improvements in the U.S. merchandise balance of trade have occurred during periods of relatively poor economic performance, whereas deteriorations have been associated with a healthy and growing domestic economy. The answer to stagnant growth and ailing industry is not to extend the damage to all other markets, but to reduce barriers to trade.

This essay has appeared previously as Canto, Victor A., Arthur B. Laffer, and James C. Turney, "Trade Policy and the U.S. Economy," *Financial Analysts Journal* September/October 1982. Reprinted with permission.

PROTECTIONISM IN THE 1980s

Protectionism is on the rise. After a decade of slow growth, nations once again are seeking to improve their trade positions in order to promote domestic prosperity. To date, the greatest impediments to trade remain within a "gray area" of trade restraints, including voluntary export restraints, orderly marketing agreements, export subsidies, and the like. In industrial sectors, such as automobiles, steel, and synthetic fibers, the following impediments to trade have been put in place:

* The unofficial, but nonetheless successful, negotiation between the United States and Japan of a voluntary export restraint limiting the number of Japanese cars exported to the United States.
* The imposition in many European countries of quotas on Japanese car imports.
* A U.S. investigation of 38 cases of alleged dumping by foreign steel suppliers, affecting 90 percent of the U.S. import volume.
* A new multifiber agreement setting tight limits on the growth of textile exports into the United States and the European Economic Community.

In addition, the Reagan administration is considering a new trade policy based on "reciprocity." The goal is to force other nations to reduce their trade barriers to U.S.-made goods and to reduce subsidies to their export industries. If a nation fails to meet the conditions, the U.S. response may be to impose restrictions and/or tariffs on its exports to the United States.

This approach represents a potentially radical change from the unconditional most-favored-nation principle that has been the foundation of trade policy among the industrial nations since 1923. In essence, this new approach requires negotiations with each trading partner before extension of the U.S. most-favored-nation (minimum) tariff structure. Under the prior system, only one negotiation was needed to ensure reduced tariffs for all. Reciprocity invites increased protectionism among the industrial countries, thus threatening a return to the beggar-thy-neighbor policies of the early 1930s.

Reciprocity is just the latest step in the steady drift in U.S. policy away from free trade (Table 7.1). Tariff rates in the United States had been on a steady downtrend since their all-time high of 59.1 percent in 1932. By the time World War II began, tariffs had decreased to 37 percent. By the war's end, tariffs had dropped to 29 percent. The first of seven rounds of trade negotiations under the auspices of the General Agreement on Tariffs and Trade commenced in 1947. By the end of the Kennedy Round of trade negotiations in 1968, tariff rates in the United States, the European Economic Community, and Japan were only about 10 percent. The Tokyo Round of trade negotiations, completed in 1978, resulted in another 30 percent reduction in tariffs, with the highest tariff rates reduced the most.

More recently, these advances toward free trade have been at least partially offset by increases in nontariff barriers. "Voluntary" quotas were imposed on steel and meat imports in 1969. In 1970 the most restrictive trade legislation since the Smoot–Hawley Tariff was passed by the House of Representatives and introduced in, but not passed by, the Senate. The year 1971 marked the final collapse of the Bretton Woods system of fixed exchange rates based on a gold standard, as the United States devalued the dollar in hopes of improving its trade balance. During the remainder of the decade, the steel import quotas were extended and then replaced with a new form of protection under a minimum pricing regulation.

The grim experience of the early 1930s amply demonstrates that this movement toward protectionism carries with it major implications for the U.S. economy. Virtually all economists and policymakers agree that, in the extreme, trade restrictions are self-defeating, impoverishing foreign countries and U.S. citizens alike. The policy issue thus centers on whether judiciously applied protectionist measures can contribute to domestic economic stability and growth. In particular, can instruments of trade policy be used to improve a country's balance of trade and thus its overall economic performance?

DEVALUATIONS, TARIFFS, AND THE TRADE BALANCE

In the early and mid-eighteenth century, European economic policy was dominated by efforts to create a favorable balance of trade as a means to increase an industrial nation's wealth. These policies (known as mercantilist) incorporated restrictions through tariffs or quotas on imports and subsidies to exports. Low wage rates also were endorsed as a means to increase exports and thereby the balance of trade.

Mercantilism associated an increase in wealth with an accumulation of precious metals. The implicit concept of the world economy was essentially one of a zero-sum game. In this static analysis, one country's gain was considered another country's loss.

TABLE 7.1. Major Changes in U.S. Trade Policy, 1930–81

Free Trade	Protectionism
	Smoot–Hawley Tariff Act of 1930 (raised agricultural raw material duties from 38 to 49%; other commodities from 31 to 34%).
Trade Agreements Act of 1934 (president authorized to negotiate U.S. trade policy; reduce specific tariffs up to 50%).	
Bilateral trade agreements with 20 nations reduced average tariffs to half their 1934 levels (1934–47).	
General Agreement on Tariffs and Trade: (1) Geneva, October 1947 (2) Annecy, France, 1949 (3) Torquay, England, September 1950 to April 1951.	
Trade Agreements Act extended (1955) for three years; Eisenhower authorized to reduce tariffs 5% a year and duties in excess of 50% ad valorem.	
	Agricultural Act of 1956 (president authorized to limit exports and agricultural imports into the United States).
	Trade Agreements Act extended (1958) four years; authorized increasing rates 50% above rates in effect on July 1, 1934.
	Quota restrictions announced (1958) on imports of lead and zinc.
	Mandatory quotas on oil imports imposed (1959).
	Established voluntary quotas on cotton textiles (1961).
	Raised tariffs on sheet glass and carpets (1962).
Trade Expansion Act of 1962 (president given authority to reduce tariffs of July 1, 1962 by 50% in five years; allowed elimination of duties on specific commodities).	Price differential for defense procurement of foreign military goods raised to 50% (1962).

(continued)

TABLE 7.1, continued

Free Trade	Protectionism
The Kennedy Round (1962) (authorized 50% tariff reductions on most industrial products and 30 to 50% on others).	Meat Import Act of 1964 (to protect domestic cattle industry).
	The Interest Equalization Tax (1964) (restricted the sale of foreign securities in the United States).
	The Voluntary Foreign Credit Restraints Program (mid-1960s) (restricted availability to foreigners of banking services in the United States).
	Foreign Direct Investment Program (mid-1960s) (restricted U.S. financing of foreign direct investments by U.S. firms).
President Johnson calls for abolition of American selling price (1968).	Negotiated voluntary quotas on steel (1968).
	Informal restraints on major meat-supplying countries (1969).
	Nixon administration submits bill to restrict textile trade (1969).
	Voluntary Restraint Agreement imposed on imports of steel (1969).
	Trade Act of 1970 passed by the House but defeated in the Senate.
	Heavier restraint on meat imposed (1970).
	Burke–Hartke Bill introduced in Senate (1971).
	President Nixon closes gold window; 10% increase in tariffs (1971).
	Tariffs on stainless-steel flatware raised (1971).
	Negotiated voluntary quotas on Mexican fruit and vegetables (1971).
	Price differential for defense procurement of foreign hand tools raised to 50% (1971).

Implementation of Kennedy Round tariff reductions completed (1972).

Trade Act of 1974 (to maintain and enlarge foreign markets).

Tokyo Round—1975 (attempted to constrain nontariff barriers).

Restraint program on meat continued (1971).

Voluntary Restraint Agreement on steel extended from 1971 to 1974 (1972).

Voluntary restraints on meat negotiated (1972).

OPEC oil embargo (1973).

U.S. soybean export embargo (1974).

Trade Act of 1974 (provided safeguards and "adjustment asistance").

Multifiber Arrangement—1974 (restricted textile imports).

Tokyo Round—1975 (implementation of safeguards and protection from international trade).

Voluntary restraint on meat negotiated (1975).

Orderly Marketing Agreement with Korea and Taiwan on nonrubber footwear (1976).

Quotas placed on specialty steel (1976).

Orderly Marketing Agreement with Japan to restrict imports of color televisions (1977).

Voluntary restrictions on meat negotiated (1977).

Shipments to the Soviet Union of wheat, superphosphoric acid embargoed (1978).

Trigger price mechanism on steel implemented (1978).

(continued)

TABLE 7.1, continued

Free Trade	Protectionism
Specialty steel quota reductions begun (July 1979), to be completed in 1980.	Restraints on imports of industrial fasteners (1979).
Trade Act of 1979 (domestic industries required to show injury by subsidized exports before offsetting duty would be imposed).	Orderly Marketing Agreement with Korea and Taiwan to restrict imports of color televisions (1980).
Orderly Marketing Agreement with Japan lapses on color televisions (1980).	25% tariff imposed on lightweight chassis (1980).
Specialty steel quotas allowed to collapse (1980).	"Voluntary" export restraint with Japan to resrict automobile imports (1980).
Embargoes on shipments to the Soviet Union of wheat, superphosphoric acid ended (1981).	Embargoes on exports requiring validated licenses for shipment to Poland and the Soviet Union (1981).
Orderly Marketing Agreement on nonrubber footwear expired (1981).	

Note: OPEC, Organization of Oil-Producing Countries.

A group of French economists—known as the Physiocrats—was among the first to challenge this mercantilist orthodoxy. Instead of emphasizing the accumulation of precious metals, they stressed the importance of increasing the aggregate level of output as the means to increase the wealth of a nation. This dynamic concept was advanced by David Hume and later by Adam Smith. Smith's classic work, *An Inquiry into the Nature and Causes of the Wealth of Nations* (1776), formed the basis of the free trade policy that became one of the hallmarks of Britain's emergence as the foremost world power during the nineteenth century.

The debate now is much the same as it was 200 years ago. The economic principles advocated by adherents to free trade can be found in the writings of Adam Smith and his predecessors. The trade account is viewed as a means to provide consumers and producers with the widest possible access to foreign goods and markets. Although restrictions placed on trade by foreign nations can be harmful to the domestic economy, imposing additional restrictions on trade at the domestic level serves only to compound the loss of economic efficiencies by limiting further opportunities to realize the benefits of trade.

By contrast, arguments today that favor increased protectionism incorporate several of the mercantilist concepts, including the importance of a positive trade balance to a nation's prosperity. Mercantilist trade policies such as currency devaluation, tariffs, and selected quotas are viewed as means to improve the trade balance and thereby the nation's wealth and prosperity. The total effect of the balance of trade on domestic income is assumed to be a multiple of any trade surplus or, moving in the opposite direction, any trade deficit—that is, a trade surplus creates a cascading series of increased expenditures (the foreign trade multiplier), while a trade deficit represents a leakage of demand from domestic to foreign goods and producers, reducing with a multiplier income and employment.

The enthusiasm for restricting trade in order to improve the domestic economy and protect selected industries is tempered today by the realization that trade restrictions can become counterproductive, impoverishing domestic and foreign producers and consumers alike. In 1930, for example, the Smoot–Hawley Tariff, which had initially aimed to protect the U.S. farmer from foreign competition and support sagging agricultural commodity prices, was, through the political process, expanded to embrace most industrial commodities as well. Between 1929 and 1931 tariffs in the United States on average were increased from 40.1 to 53.2 percent. Tariffs on dutiable imports peaked one year later, hitting an all-time high of 59.1 percent. The economic events accompanying the passage of this tariff were dramatic. As the bill advanced in the Senate in 1929, the stock market began its historic sell-off, including the crash of October 29, 1929. In 1930 gross national product (GNP)—after adjustment for a decline in the price level— fell by 9.5 percent, wiping out three years of growth and initiating the Great Depression. Ironically, farm commodity prices and employment fell that year, as did the standard of living of most U.S. citizens.

Thus, as concern about international competitiveness and protectionist sentiment in the United States have increased, alternatives to across-the-board increases in tariffs have been sought. Among the most popular of these alternatives is the devaluation of the dollar. Devaluation does not interfere directly with trade or invite retaliation from U.S. trading partners and offers the promise of reducing the price of U.S. goods in world markets, thus increasing the U.S. economy's competitive strength.

CURRENCY DEVALUATION

The goal of currency devaluation is to change the prices of goods in one country relative to another by changing the relationship between the currencies in which prices in each country are measured.

Advocates of devaluation observe that, following devaluation of the domestic currency, the prices of foreign currencies and therefore foreign-produced goods will be higher for domestic citizens. At the same time, the price of the domestic currency and therefore domestically produced goods will become lower to foreigners. The rise in the prices of imported goods will bring about a reduction in the level of imports. And the lower prices of goods exported to foreigners will increase the level of exports. With fewer imports and a stimulus to exports, the trade balance of the devaluing country will improve. Thus, devaluation should increase the competitiveness of the U.S. economy and improve its trade balance.

A study by Richard Cooper (1971a,b) lent support to those who argued for devaluation of the U.S. dollar. His analysis of 24 devaluations effected by 19 countries during the 1959–66 period showed that, in 15 of the 24 episodes, an improvement in the balance of goods and services occurred the year following devaluation.

The U.S. experience with a depreciating currency, however, has not produced such a happy result. Between 1970 and 1978, the value of the dollar relative to the currencies of eight industrial countries (Canada, France, Germany, Italy, Japan, the Netherlands, Switzerland, and the

United Kingdom) fell by 24.1 percent. Yet the country's merchandise trade balance went from a $2.6 billion *surplus* in 1970 to a record $33.8 billion *deficit* in 1978. Even in 1972—the year after the United States first devalued by 10 percent—the merchandise trade balance slipped from a $2.3 billion deficit to a $6.4 billion deficit.

Although anecdotal, the experience of the United States is consistent with numerous, more extensive research since the Cooper study analyzing the ability of changes in exchange rates to affect the trade balance. In 1977, for example, Arthur Laffer examined the effects of 15 postwar devaluations over a period of several years, rather than only the year following devaluation.[1] Analyzing the path of the trade balance over seven years (three years prior to the year of devaluation and three years after), Laffer found that the trade balance tended on average to worsen. Ten of 15 countries experienced the largest deficits of the seven-year period in the three years following devaluation; two more countries had the largest deficits during the year of devaluation. In 11 of the 14 instances where data were available, the deficits were larger in the third year following devaluation, and in 8 out of 14 cases the deficits were larger in the second year following devaluation than one year before. Laffer concludes that there is little evidence that devaluation caused significant or sustained improvement in the trade balance.

These results were confirmed by a follow-up study by Michael Salant (1977), using Laffer's data. The major difference between the studies was that whereas Laffer measured trade balances in terms of the country's domestic currency, Salant chose to measure the trade balance in a common foreign currency (dollars). Following devaluation, the trade balance may move in one direction as measured in domestic currency and in the opposite direction as measured in foreign currency. Salant found that, in 8 of the 15 episodes of devaluation, the trade balance improved in the three years after devaluation as compared with the three years preceding. Laffer's study (domestic currency) indicated that the trade balance improved in only 6 of the 15 episodes. Salant concluded that the slight increase in the number of cases is not large enough to upset Laffer's conclusions: Currency devaluation has little or no effect on the trade balance, whether measured in domestic or foreign currency terms.

Salant conducted a more extensive study of 101 devaluations by developed and less-developed countries. Of the 23 devaluations by developed countries, the trade balance improved in 8 instances and worsened in 15. Of the 78 devaluations in less-developed countries, the trade balance improved in 38 and worsened in 39 instances (staying unchanged in 1). In total, the balance of trade improved in 46 episodes of devaluation, worsened in 54, and did not change in 1. Salant's results indicate that devaluations more often than not lead to deterioration in the trade balance—not improvement.[2]

Figure 7.1 provides additional evidence concerning the relationship between the trade balance and currency exchange rates using data for 11 major industrialized countries. Changes in the trade balance are represented by changes in the net export ratio—the trade balance of a particular country divided by the total production of the country. A positive change represents a tendency toward surplus in the merchandise balance of trade. A negative change in the net export ratio indicates that imports are growing faster than exports (a trend toward a trade balance deficit for the country). Changes in the exchange rates of ten domestic currencies relative to the U.S. dollar are shown in percentage terms.[3] Positive exchange rate changes represent appreciation of the local currency; negative changes indicate depreciation relative to the U.S. dollar. The relationships are plotted for two annual changes, 1977–78 and 1978–79.

No systematic relationship is evident between changes in exchange rates and changes in merchandise trade balances. During 1978 trade balance improvements were more often than not associated with currency appreciation. The results for 1979 were largely in the opposite direction. However, the major devaluing country—Japan—registered the largest trade deterioration in 1979.

One explanation for the inability of a devaluation to improve the trade balance is that the economies of the United States and its trading partners are fully integrated into a single market. Imagine, for example, that after a 10 percent devaluation of the dollar, the price of wheat in Chicago falls 10 percent below the price of wheat in London. At that spread, trading companies will be willing to buy up the entire U.S. wheat crop. As a result, the price differential is dissipated almost immediately.

What is true for wheat and other raw materials also is true on average for all other goods and services in the economy. After the price of wheat rises by 10 percent to reach equilibrium with the world price, the value of the land it is grown on can be expected to rise an equivalent amount. In this way, the change in the value of the basic commodity prices tends to permeate the entire price level. The net result is that the sought-after positive effects of devaluation are, in short order, fully offset by higher relative inflation in the devaluing country.

This process is not reflected immediately in consumer or wholesale price indexes. But over a period of a year and longer, this "Law of One

FIGURE 7.1. Trade Balance and Exchange Rate Changes[a]

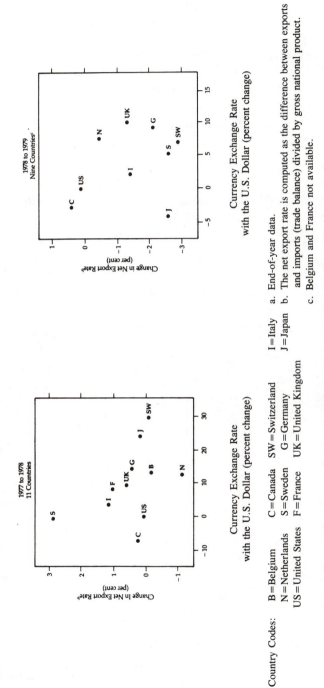

Country Codes:

B = Belgium	C = Canada	SW = Switzerland	I = Italy
N = Netherlands	S = Sweden	G = Germany	J = Japan
US = United States	F = France	UK = United Kingdom	

a. End-of-year data.
b. The net export rate is computed as the difference between exports and imports (trade balance) divided by gross national product.
c. Belgium and France not available.

Source: International Financial Statistics, Bureau of Statistics of the International Monetary Fund. Washington, D.C.

Price'' becomes evident. For example, a comparison of annual changes in the U.S. wholesale price index with changes in the British wholesale price index converted to its U.S. dollar equivalent (thereby taking into account any changes in exchange rates) shows an extremely close correlation from 1900 to the present (Graph 7.1) Comparisons of the wholesale price index of other industrial countries from Japan to France produce similar results.

Even if the terms of trade were to change as a consequence of devaluation, the devaluationist model is logically inconsistent. Suppose that the

GRAPH 7.1. Wholesale Price Inflation in the United States and Britain (Both Measured in U.S. Dollars), 1901–81

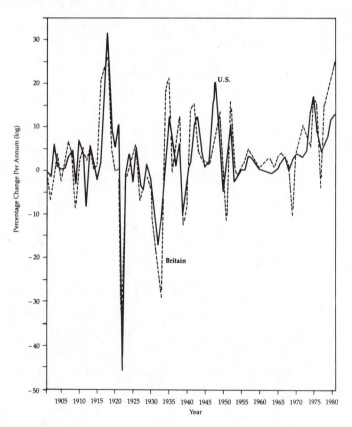

Sources: The Golden Constant, Roy Jastram. 1977. New York: John Wiley and Sons; *International Financial Statistics*, Bureau of Statistics of the International Monetary Fund. Washington, D.C.

devaluing country's exportable goods are made less expensive (relative to its importables). Residents of the devaluing country now want to buy more of these less expensive export goods, leaving less for export. But, in order for the trade balance to improve, *more* of the goods must be shipped to foreigners, *not less*. At the same time, the exportable goods of the country whose currency has risen in value (the devaluing country's importables) are made more expensive. As a result, residents of the country devalued against want to buy fewer of their now-more-expensive export goods, leaving more for export. But in order for the trade balance of the devaluing country to improve, the country whose currency has risen in value must export *less, not more.*

TARIFFS AND QUOTAS

Import tariffs and export subsidies represent another set of policies used to improve the balance of trade. Advocates of these policies observe that tariffs raise the domestic prices of imported goods and subsidies reduce the prices of products exported to foreigners. This reduction in imports and the stimulus to exports are believed to improve the balance of trade and consequently domestic economic conditions.

An analysis of the effects of changes in average tariff rates on the trade balance, however, indicates that the real world effects of tariffs on the balance of trade are more complex. Not only do tariffs reduce imports, but they are associated with a decline in exports as well. Thus, the impact of tariffs on the trade balance is ambiguous (with the exception of the extreme case in which a country running a trade balance deficit bans all imports).

The effects of tariffs for 11 major industrialized countries are examined empirically here by analyzing the correlation over time between tariff and import levels. Import tariffs are represented by the average tariff rate collected, computed by dividing the revenues received by government from customs and duties by the volume of imports.[4]

Import tariffs are related to both imports and exports (see Figures 7.2 to 7.5). The correlations between the average tariff rates and imports are negative in the majority of countries. An increase in tariffs is associated with a decline in imports. But exports, too, are associated negatively with import tariffs in the majority of countries—that is, an increase in import tariffs is associated with a decline in exports. The decline in exports and imports indicates that the overall volume of trade is reduced by tariffs.

Moreover, since both exports and imports are reduced by import tariffs, trade balance (exports less imports) would be little changed. In fact, the statistical tests provide little or no evidence that trade balances are affected by tariffs (Table 7.2).

These results indicate that the policies of explicit tariffs and quasi-tariffs (such as the increasingly popular trigger pricing mechanisms) are largely *ineffective* in changing the trade balance.[5] This result can be understood by realizing that exports and imports are two sides of the same transaction: The object of producing goods for export is to be able to import and consume goods produced by foreigners. Producers and machines do not devote their work effort in order to acquire British pounds sterling and Japanese yen for their aesthetic appeal. The foreign currencies are exchanged for foreign goods to be imported or for foreign bonds, claims to future goods. The raison d'être for exporting is per se importing, either now or in the future.

FIGURE 7.2. German Tariff Rate Versus Imports and Exports

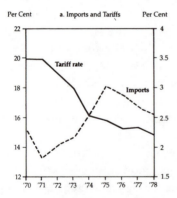 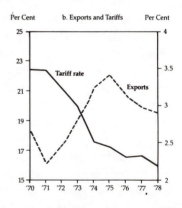

_____ Average tariff rate collected, computed as tariff and customs revenue divided by merchandise imports.
------ Ratio of merchandise imports to gross national product.

_____ Average tariff rate collected, computed as tariff and customs revenue divided by merchandise imports.
------ Ratio of merchandise exports to gross national product.

Sources: *International Financial Statistics*, Bureau of Statistics of the International Monetary Fund. Washington, D.C.; *OECD Revenue Statistics*, Department of Economics and Statistics, Organization for Economic Co-operation and Development. Paris, France.

FIGURE 7.3. Japanese Tariff Rate Versus Imports and Exports

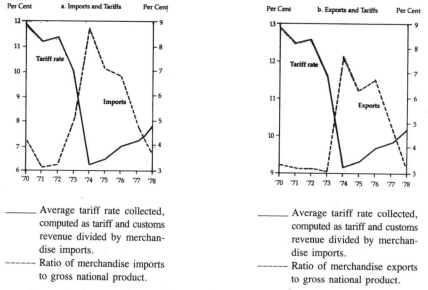

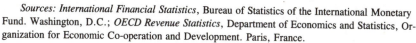

——— Average tariff rate collected, computed as tariff and customs revenue divided by merchandise imports.

------ Ratio of merchandise imports to gross national product.

——— Average tariff rate collected, computed as tariff and customs revenue divided by merchandise imports.

------ Ratio of merchandise exports to gross national product.

Sources: International Financial Statistics, Bureau of Statistics of the International Monetary Fund. Washington, D.C.; *OECD Revenue Statistics*, Department of Economics and Statistics, Organization for Economic Co-operation and Development. Paris, France.

Suppose that a tariff successfully reduces the volume of imports by one-half. There are now only half as many foreign goods available to exchange for domestically produced goods, given the world terms of trade. So the volume of exports must be reduced symmetrically by one-half. The net effect on the trade balance? None. A tax on imports is equivalent in effect to a tax on exports. This principle is referred to as Lerner's Symmetry Theorem, a well-known principle of trade theory (see Lerner 1936).

Quantitative restrictions in the form of import quotas and self-imposed foreign export quotas also are on the menu of protectionist policies. In principle, there is a precise correspondence between quotas and tariffs: For any quota (or quantitative restriction) imposed, there exists a tariff that will produce exactly the same price effects and quantity effects on imports and exports. The Lerner Symmetry Theorem is equally applicable to quotas: A restriction on imports is equivalent to a restriction on exports and can be expected to have little or no effect on the balance of trade.

FIGURE 7.4. U.K. Tariff Rate Versus Imports and Exports

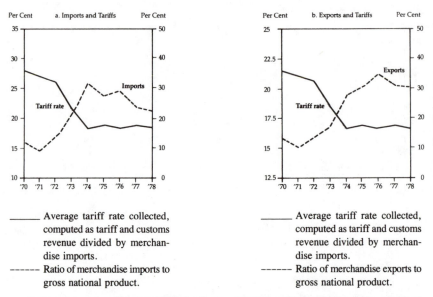

_____ Average tariff rate collected,
computed as tariff and customs
revenue divided by merchandise imports.

------ Ratio of merchandise imports to
gross national product.

_____ Average tariff rate collected,
computed as tariff and customs
revenue divided by merchandise imports.

------ Ratio of merchandise exports to
gross national product.

Sources: International Financial Statistics, Bureau of Statistics of the International Monetary Fund. Washington, D.C.; *OECD Revenue Statistics*, Department of Economics and Statistics, Organization for Economic Co-operation and Development. Paris, France.

Thus, the efficacy of protectionist measures in terms of improving the trade balance is dubious on both theoretical and empirical grounds. Trade restrictions do, however, impair the efficiency of the world economy and reduce the standard of living of individuals in all trading nations. To the extent that trade restrictions are effective, the gains from trade in both production and consumption are lost.[6] Production incentives shift away from those goods produced more efficiently domestically.[7] And consumers are no longer able to choose goods produced more efficiently abroad.

Trade restrictions devised to protect a particular industry may well accomplish that task for a period of time. But the cost of protecting that industry is borne by the rest of the economy. Tariffs and quotas on imports constitute tax wedges for the world economy. With fewer goods available at higher prices in each domestic economy, the rewards for work effort are reduced. Often, the resulting decline in economic activity

FIGURE 7.5. U.S. Tariff Rate Versus Imports and Exports

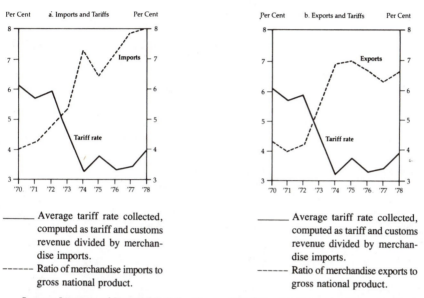

—————— Average tariff rate collected, computed as tariff and customs revenue divided by merchandise imports.

－－－－－ Ratio of merchandise imports to gross national product.

—————— Average tariff rate collected, computed as tariff and customs revenue divided by merchandise imports.

－－－－－ Ratio of merchandise exports to gross national product.

Sources: International Financial Statistics, Bureau of Statistics of the International Monetary Fund. Washington, D.C.; *OECD Revenue Statistics*, Department of Economics and Statistics, Organization for Economic Co-operation and Development. Paris, France.

reduces the standard of living of workers in protected and unprotected industries alike, leaving all worse off.

THE BALANCE OF TRADE

The central tenet of much of the effort to improve the balance of trade is the belief that a trade surplus is indicative of a healthy economy with rising income and employment. This belief, however, is contradicted by the experience of the United States and other countries.

Between 1790 and 1875 the U.S. merchandise trade account was in deficit for 74 years (Graph 7.2). Yet U.S. output increased enormously. During the post-World War II era, improvements in the U.S. trade account have typically occurred during years of relatively poorer, not better, economic performance. In addition, periods of above-average growth have been associated with a deterioration (not an improvement) in the trade account.

TABLE 7.2. Tariffs and the Trade Balance, 1970–78[a]

	Correlation of a Change in Tariff Rates With[b]		
	Change in Ratio of Imports and GNP	Change in Ratio of Exports and GNP	Change in Ratio of Trade Balance and GNP
Belgium	−0.55	−0.63	−0.15
	(−1.63)	(−1.99)[c]	(−0.37)
Canada	−0.19	−0.13	−0.06
	(−0.49)	(−0.32)	(0.16)
France	0.14	0.01	−0.22
	(0.36)	(0.01)	(0.54)
Germany	−0.59	−0.76	−0.56
	(−0.78)	(−2.84)[c]	(−1.68)
Italy	−0.13	0.15	0.21
	(−0.31)	(0.36)	(0.54)
Japan	−0.89	−0.87	0.52
	(−4.84)[c]	(−4.25)[c]	(1.50)
Netherlands	−0.47	−0.35	0.25
	(−1.30)	(−0.91)	(0.62)
Sweden	−0.74	−0.46	0.49
	(−2.67)[c]	(−1.25)	(1.37)
Switzerland	0.08	0.60	0.77
	(0.19)	(1.83)[c]	(2.93)[c]
United Kingdom	−0.88	−0.60	0.91
	(−4.45)[c]	(−1.84)[c]	(5.29)[c]
United States	−0.70	−0.70	0.08
	(−2.38)[c]	(−2.41)[c]	(0.19)

a. Tariff rate equals the ratio of government revenues from customs and duties to imports.

b. A correction of −1.0 means two variables are perfectly, negatively correlated; a correlation of 0.0 means two variables are not correlated; a correlation of 1.0 means two variables are perfectly, positively correlated.

c. Statistically significant.

Sources: International Financial Statistics, Bureau of Statistics of the International Monetary Fund. Washington, D.C.; *OECD Revenue Statistics*, Department of Economics and Statistics, Organization for Economic Co-operation and Development. Paris, France.

The relationship between the merchandise trade balance and economic growth was analyzed for 11 industrial countries. (The merchandise trade balance is the difference between merchandise exports and merchandise imports.) Trade balances were computed as a share of GNP. Each country's economic performance relative to the other ten countries was computed using the real GNP growth of the subject country less the real growth rate of the aggregate GNP of the other ten countries.[8]

GRAPH 7.2. U.S. Trade Balance, 1790–1875

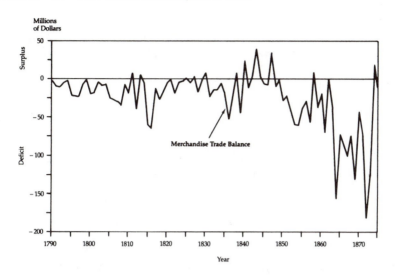

Source: Historical Statistics of the United States: Colonial Times to 1970, U.S. Department of Commerce, Bureau of the Census. Government Printing Office. Washington, D.C.

Six of the 11 countries—Canada, Italy, Japan, Switzerland, the United Kingdom, and the United States—exhibited a negative relationship between their relative growth rates and their trade balances (Table 7.3). This means that years of above-average growth rates in output relative to the world were associated with a *decline* in the trade balance—that is, a deterioration, not an improvement, in the trade account was a sign of a healthy, growing economy demanding resources from the rest of the world. For three of the remaining countries—Belgium, France, and Sweden—the improvement in the trade account was symptomatic of an acceleration in growth relative to the world. In only one country, the Netherlands, were the results not statistically significant. For another, Germany, the results were ambiguous—that is, the leads were positive, while the lags were negative.

The evidence suggests that trade deficits, or deteriorations in the trade balance, are desirable more often than not. Alarm and concern over rising net imports typically are unfounded. And efforts to correct trade balance deficits, if successful, often stifle rather than augment domestic economic growth.

The relationship between economic growth and the trade balance can

TABLE 7.3. The Trade Balance and Economic Growth

Direction of Statistically Significant Relations[a]

Positive	Negative	Ambiguous	Not Statistically Significant
Belgium	Canada	Germany[b]	Netherlands
France	Italy		
Sweden	Japan		
	Switzerland		
	U.K.		
	U.S.		

a. Using the 5 percent level of significance (see Appendix for detail).
b. Leading positive, lagging negative.

be better understood by viewing the economies of the United States and its trading partners as fully integrated in a single, global economy. From the perspective of the global economy, the relevant market is the integrated world market—not a collection of multiple markets in isolation Single world market equilibrium prices and quantities will be determined by worldwide supply and demand conditions. Global equilibrium requires that there be only one worldwide price at which the supply of goods equals the demand for goods.[9]

Given worldwide equilibrium and prices, local equilibrium in any specific country is not only unnecessary, but highly improbable. Local disequilibrium can be satisfied by trade in goods; excess supplies can be exported and excess demands satisfied by imports. In the global model, therefore, a trade balance surplus indicates that the local economy produced more goods than it consumed at going world prices. Conversely, a deficit in the balance of trade implies that the country demanded more goods than it supplied, at going world prices.

The trade account can be viewed as the means by which an aggregate economy can adjust its temporal pattern of consumption and investment, on the one hand, and production and savings, on the other. During most of the United States' first century, for example, investment opportunities exceeded the domestic economy's aggregate savings. Stated differently, during this period more goods and services (consumption) and capital goods (investment) were acquired than were produced. The difference was the net imports from the rest of the world, as foreign suppliers provided the excess goods, services, and capital goods in exchange for future claims (bonds and stocks) against the output of the U.S. economy. Conversely, in the 1950s investment opportunities in rebuilding Europe and Japan exceeded those economies' savings and production relative to their consumption. The United States ran a trade balance surplus and invested heavily in foreign nations.

Conceivably, any supply shock or demand shock to a specific country or to the rest of the world can produce a trade phenomenon. For example, if an economy suddenly contracts along with a sharp fall in demand, its trade account may improve. Conversely, an improvement in the trade account may accompany a sharp increase in output and economic growth relative to demand. Thus, an improvement in the trade account may be the result of deterioration as well as improvement in a country's overall economic condition. The trade account in isolation, however, is of little value as an indicator of the health of an economy.

CONCLUSION

Trade policies have always captured the imagination of government employees and academic scribblers. Time after time, the hopes of thrifty capitalists and hard-working laborers have been primed by protectionists' promises. The lessons from history, both of the recent past and ancient times, have far too frequently been ignored, resulting in impoverishment on a global scale.

Tariffs and quotas are as pernicious policy options as ever created. Their popularity stems exclusively from their ready availability and misguided theory. The oversight of international trade requires but a small bureaucracy in comparison with the oversight of, say, intraregional transactions. Basic xenophobia has contributed to the disregard of, if not outright disdain for, foreign interests. Both on grounds of ease of interference and political appeal of discrimination, restrictive trade practices have thrived since the dawning of civilization. Great thinkers, no matter how careful and well documented their logic, have often been unable to protect the electorate from the noxious rhetoric of political demagogues.

Protectionist measures not only do not work, but actually harm those who use them. Steelworkers are being sold a bill of goods in believing that antidumping, countervailing duties and trigger price mechanisms are designed in a way that will help them. They are, ironically, the innocent victims of political exploitation. Rarely is anyone made better off by pulling another down. The results could not be clearer.

Political pundits and word merchants have deflected the true course of logic and misdirected criticism to linguistically defenseless and politically impotent foreigners. The answer to stagnant growth and ailing industries in the United States and Europe is not to extend the damage to all other market participants. The solution lies in curing the unwarranted pain and hardship conferred on the industrialized economy through corrective legislation that reduces the barriers to trade—whether it be with the merchant down the block, across town, or halfway around the world.

APPENDIX
THE MERCHANDISE TRADE BALANCE
AND ECONOMIC GROWTH

In the regression equations examining the relationship between the merchandise trade balance and economic growth, the dependent variable is the change in the trade balance as a share of GNP; the explanatory variable is the growth rate differential. The basic relationship is examined incorporating leading and lagging growth rate differentials in addition to the concurrent relationship. The trade effects of the 1974 oil price shock are considered by two alternative methods: In the first method, a dummy variable (0–1 type) is incorporated; in the second, 1974 is deleted from the time series sample to avoid reporting inflated R^2 values resulting from the dummy variable method.

The following definitions are used:

Δ = the annual change in the variable

$\dfrac{TB}{GNP}$ = the net export ratio, computed as the merchandise trade balance of the country divided by its GNP, expressed in U.S. dollars

g_i = the real GNP growth for the country, computed as the percentage change in its GNP expressed in 1975 dollars

g_{row} = the real GNP growth for the rest of the world, computed as the percentage change in the aggregate GNP of the other ten countries in the sample, expressed in 1975 dollars

D = a dummy variable to consider the OPEC price increase in 1974; D is equal to 1 in 1974 and to 0 in all other years.

The equations are as follow:

Concurrent

$$\Delta\left(\frac{TB}{GNP}\right)=b_0+b_1\Delta(g_i-g_{row})_t+e \tag{1}$$

$$\Delta\left(\frac{TB}{GNP}\right)=b_0+b_1\Delta(g_i-g_{row})_t+e \text{ (1974 deleted)} \tag{2}$$

$$\Delta\left(\frac{TB}{GNP}\right)=b_0+b_1\Delta(g_i-g_{row})_t+b_3D+e \tag{3}$$

Lagging

$$\Delta\left(\frac{TB}{GNP}\right)=b_0+b_1\Delta(g_i-g_{row})_t+b_2\Delta(g_i-g_{row})_{t-1}+e \tag{4}$$

$$\Delta\left(\frac{TB}{GNP}\right)=b_0+b_1\Delta(g_i-g_{row})_t+b_2\Delta(g_i-g_{row})_{t-1}+e \text{ (1974 deleted)} \tag{5}$$

$$\Delta\left(\frac{TB}{GNP}\right)=b_0+b_1\Delta(g_i-g_{row})_t+b_2\Delta(g_i-g_{row})_{t-1}+b_3D+e \tag{6}$$

Leading

$$\Delta\left(\frac{TB}{GNP}\right)=b_0+b_1\Delta(g_i-g_{row})_t+b_2\Delta(g_i-g_{row})_{t+1}+e \tag{7}$$

$$\Delta\left(\frac{TB}{GNP}\right)=b_0+b_1\Delta(g_i-g_{row})_t+b_2\Delta(g_i-g_{row})_{t+1}+e \text{ (1974 deleted)} \tag{8}$$

$$\Delta\left(\frac{TB}{GNP}\right)=b_0+b_1\Delta(g_i-g_{row})_t+b_2\Delta(g_i-g_{row})_{t+1}+b_3D+e \tag{9}$$

Lagging and Leading

$$\Delta\left(\frac{TB}{GNP}\right)=b_0+b_1\Delta(g_i-g_{row})_{t-1}+b_2\Delta(g_i-g_{row})_t+ \\ b_3\Delta(g_i-g_{row})_{t+1}+e. \tag{10}$$

Equations 2, 5, and 8 duplicate Equations 1, 4, and 7, respectively, but delete 1974 to consider the OPEC price increase effects.

Tables 7A.1 to 7A.11 give the results of these equations for Belgium, Canada, France, Germany, Italy, Japan, the Netherlands, Sweden, Switzerland, the United Kingdom, and the United States. (Equation 10 is estimated for Canada and Germany only.) The t-statistics are shown in parentheses, and results of the F tests and Durbin–Watson tests are shown in the penultimate and antepenultimate columns. The last column gives the number of observations used in estimating each equation and the time period covered.

TABLE 7A.1. Merchandise Trade Balance and Economic Growth: Germany

Equation	b_0	b_1	b_2	b_3	R^2	F	DW	# Observations Dates
1	-0.00056 (-0.328)	-0.00093 (-1.199)			0.06	1.44	1.69	23 57–79
2	-0.00102 (-0.589)	-0.00117 (-1.418)			0.09	2.01	1.89	22 57–79
3	-0.00102 (-0.589)	-0.00117 (-1.418)		0.01017 (1.210)	0.13	1.47	1.69	23 57–79
4	-0.00095 (-0.594)	-0.00088 (-1.151)	-0.00159 (-2.051)		0.23	2.93	1.87	23 57–79
5	-0.00147 (-0.922)	-0.00108 (-1.430)	-0.00166 (-2.192)		0.27	3.60	2.04	22 57–79
6	-0.00147 (-0.922)	-0.00108 (-1.430)	-0.00166 (-2.192)	0.01121 (1.452)	0.30	2.76	1.90	23 57–79
7	0.00013 (0.087)	-0.00077 (-1.060)	0.00169 (2.387)		0.26	3.28	2.01	22 57–78
8	-0.00042 (-0.281)	-0.00101 (-1.411)	0.00183 (2.652)		0.32	4.24	2.22	21 57–78
9	-0.00042 (-0.281)	-0.00101 (-1.411)	0.00183 (2.652)	0.01132 (1.578)	0.35	3.19	1.97	22 57–78
10	-0.00015 (-0.095)	-0.00089 (-1.117)	-0.00071 (-0.982)	0.00131 (1.668)	0.30	2.63	2.04	22 57–78

Note: For Germany, the trade balance and growth rate differential are related significantly. However, the direction (positive or negative) is ambiguous. The concurrent relationship is not statistically significant in any of the equations, nor is the oil dummy variable. The coefficients of lagging growth rate differentials are statistically significant and negative. The leading coefficients are significant and positive. Regressing the leading and lagging growth rate differentials in combination failed to produce statistically significant results.

115

TABLE 7A.2. Merchandise Trade Balance and Economic Growth: Italy

Equation	b_0	b_1	b_2	b_3	R^2	F	DW	# Observations Dates
1	0.00174 (0.6.56)	−0.00317 (−3.666)			0.35	13.44	1.83	27 53–79
2	0.00241 (0.907)	−0.00296 (−3.420)			0.33	11.69	2.12	26 53–79
3	0.00241 (0.907)	−0.00296 (−3.420)		−0.01881 (−1.338)	0.39	7.83	1.89	27 53–79
4	0.00058 (0.226)	−0.00415 (−4.235)	−0.00007 (−0.082)		0.47	10.22	1.67	26 54–79
5	0.00127 (0.488)	−0.00376 (−3.647)	0.00027 (0.288)		0.44	8.81	1.91	25 54–79
6	0.00127 (0.488)	−0.00376 (−3.647)	0.00027 (0.288)	−0.01615 (−1.135)	0.50	7.33	1.73	26 54–79
7	0.00208 (0.753)	−0.00276 (−2.841)	0.00100 (0.944)		0.35	6.32	1.85	26 53–78
8	0.00263 (0.932)	−0.00274 (−2.819)	0.00047 (0.392)		0.31	4.90	2.15	25 53–78
9	0.00263 (0.932)	−0.00274 (−2.819)	0.00047 (0.392)	−0.01644 (−1.005)	0.38	4.55	1.89	26 53–78

Note: The relationship between the trade balance and the growth rate differential for Italy is negative. Neither the leading nor lagging growth rate differentials enter the equations significantly. The 1974 oil price shock does not appear to have affected the trade balance significantly. The concurrent relationship is signficant and negative in all equations.

116

TABLE 7A.3. Merchandise Trade Balance and Economic Growth: Japan

Equation	b_0	b_1	b_2	b_3	R^2	F	DW	# Observations Dates
1	0.00017 (0.072)	-0.00141 (-2.354)			0.26	5.54	1.62	18 62–79
2	0.00090 (0.384)	-0.00164 (-2.722)			0.33	7.41	2.18	17 62–79
3	0.00090 (0.384)	-0.00164 (-2.722)		-0.01465 (-1.424)	0.35	3.96	1.80	18 62–79
4	-0.00012 (-0.051)	-0.00165 (-2.443)	-0.00055 (-0.808)		0.29	3.04	1.53	18 62–79
5	0.00061 (0.259)	-0.00198 (-2.913)	-0.00069 (-1.063)		0.38	4.30	1.98	17 62–79
6	0.00061 (0.259)	-0.00198 (-2.913)	-0.00069 (-1.063)	-0.01623 (-1.567)	0.39	3.04	1.66	18 62–79
7	0.00148 (0.688)	-0.00108 (-1.799)	0.00049 (0.715)		0.31	3.13	1.88	17 62–78
8	0.00237 (1.169)	0.00127 (-2.270)	0.00067 (1.061)		0.44	5.07	2.81	16 62–78
9	0.00237 (1.169)	-0.00127 (-2.270)	0.00067 (1.061)	-0.01681 (-1.927)	0.46	3.73	2.31	17 62–78

Note: For Japan the trade balance and growth rate differential are related negatively. Both the lagging and leading growth rate differentials failed to contribute significantly to the regressions. The concurrent relationship is significant and negative in all equations. In Equation 3, the oil dummy variable did not enter significantly.

117

TABLE 7A.4. Merchandise Trade Balance and Economic Growth: Netherlands

Equation	b_0	b_1	b_2	b_3	R^2	F	DW	# Observations Dates
1	0.00105 (0.418)	−0.00178 (−1.700)			0.15	2.89	1.86	18 62–79
2	0.00127 (0.478)	−0.00163 (−1.402)			0.12	1.97	1.87	17 62–79
3	0.00127 (0.478)	−0.00163 (−1.402)		−0.00412 (−0.339)	0.16	1.42	1.84	18 62–79
4	0.00073 (0.269)	−0.00200 (−1.706)	−0.00072 (−0.610)		0.17	1.46	1.74	17 63–79
5	0.00081 (0.279)	−0.00193 (−1.401)	−0.00067 (−0.515)		0.13	0.99	1.75	16 63–79
6	0.00081 (0.279)	−0.00193 (−1.401)	−0.00067 (−0.515)	−0.00146 (−0.106)	0.17	0.91	1.73	17 63–79
7	0.00096 (0.350)	−0.00184 (−1.528)	−0.00017 (−0.097)		0.15	1.28	1.77	17 62–78
8	0.00128 (0.431)	−0.00171 (−1.324)	−0.00030 (−0.224)		0.12	0.88	1.75	16 62–78
9	0.00128 (0.431)	−0.00171 (−1.324)	−0.00030 (−0.224)	−0.00516 (−0.365)	0.16	0.84	1.71	17 62–78

Note: For the Netherlands no statistically significant ($\alpha = 0.05$) results were revealed in the relation of the trade balance to the growth rate differential.

TABLE 7A.5. Merchandise Trade Balance and Economic Growth: Canada

Equation	b_0	b_1	b_2	b_3	R^2	F	DW	# Observations Dates
1	0.00062 (0.279)	0.00071 (0.909)			0.03	0.83	2.39	28 52–79
2	0.00112 (0.502)	0.00086 (1.091)			0.05	1.19	2.54	27 52–79
3	0.00112 (0.502)	0.00086 (1.091)		−0.01420 (−1.183)	0.08	1.12	2.52	28 52–79
4	0.00037 (0.203)	−0.00020 (−0.292)	−0.00251 (−3.678)		0.37	7.38	2.06	28 52–79
5	0.00075 (0.403)	−0.00007 (−0.094)	−0.00243 (−3.549)		0.37	7.17	2.12	27 52–79
6	0.00075 (0.403)	−0.00007 (−0.094)	−0.00243 (−3.549)	−0.01035 (−1.037)	0.40	5.29	2.21	28 52–79
7	0.00115 (0.526)	0.00126 (1.581)	0.00181 (2.046)		0.18	2.55	1.94	27 52–78
8	0.00165 (0.752)	0.00140 (1.750)	0.00179 (2.037)		0.19	2.73	2.04	26 52–78
9	0.00165 (0.752)	0.00140 (1.750)	0.00179 (2.037)	−0.01381 (−1.199)	0.22	2.21	2.06	27 52–78
10	0.00038 (0.194)	−0.00244 (−2.680)	−0.00013 (−0.150)	0.00015 (0.145)	0.37	4.53	2.03	27 52–78

Note: The relationship between the trade balance and the growth rate differential for Canada is negative. The concurrent relationship alone is not statistically significant, and the 1974 oil price shock does not enter any of the equations significantly. With lagged growth, the relationship is negative. With leading growth, the sign of the coefficient is positive. Regressing the leading and lagging growth rate differentials in combination, the lagged term dominates, while the leading coefficient is not statistically significant (the correlation between the leading and lagging variables is −0.42). The lagged term in Equation 10 remains significant and is negative.

119

TABLE 7A.6. Merchandise Trade Balance and Economic Growth: France

Equation	b_0	b_1	b_2	b_3	R^2	F	DW	# Observations Dates
1	-0.0101 (-0.341)	-0.00189 (-1.367)			0.16	1.87	2.72	12 68-79
2	0.00079 (0.245)	-0.00050 (-0.285)			0.01	0.08	3.01	11 68-79
3	0.00079 (0.245)	-0.00050 (-0.285)		-0.01654 (-1.229)	0.28	1.74	2.82	12 68-79
4	-0.00063 (-0.262)	-0.00070 (-0.569)	0.00306 (2.450)		0.49	4.40	2.48	12 68-79
5	0.00149 (0.629)	0.00100 (0.727)	0.00327 (2.983)		0.53	4.53	2.12	11 68-79
6	0.00149 (0.629)	0.00100 (0.727)	0.00327 (2.983)	-0.01933 (-1.960)	0.66	5.14	2.18	12 68-79
7	-0.00057 (-0.179)	-0.00263 (-1.638)	-0.00128 (-0.781)		0.25	1.36	2.71	11 68-78
8	0.00115 (0.335)	-0.00122 (-0.624)	-0.00151 (-0.942)		0.13	0.54	2.97	10 68-78
9	0.00115 (0.335)	-0.00122 (-0.624)	-0.00151 (-0.942)	-0.01717 (-1.208)	0.38	1.45	2.97	11 68-78

Note: The relationship of the trade balance of France with the growth rate differential is positive. None of the concurrent coefficients is statistically significant, nor are the leading relationships. The coefficients of the lagged growth rate differentials are significant and positive. In Equation 6, the oil dummy variable contributes significantly to the equation.

TABLE 7A.7. Merchandise Trade Balance and Economic Growth: Sweden

Equation	b_0	b_1	b_2	b_3	R^2	F	DW	# Observations Dates
1	0.00025 (0.104)	-0.00031 (-0.454)			0.01	0.21	2.64	26 54-79
2	0.00189 (0.970)	0.00057 (0.986)			0.04	0.97	2.09	25 54-79
3	0.00189 (0.970)	0.00057 (0.986)		-0.04330 (-4.057)	0.42	8.40	2.17	26 54-79
4	0.00024 (0.098)	-0.00052 (-0.733)	-0.00070 (-1.056)		0.05	0.66	2.85	26 54-79
5	0.00183 (0.928)	0.00045 (0.722)	-0.00035 (-0.607)		0.06	0.66	2.19	25 54-79
6	0.00183 (0.928)	0.00045 (0.722)	-0.00035 (-0.607)	-0.04207 (-3.821)	0.43	5.57	2.31	26 54-79
7	0.00123 (0.523)	0.00015 (0.218)	0.00103 (1.457)		0.09	1.09	2.61	25 54-78
8	0.00312 (1.948)	0.00112 (2.274)	0.00102 (2.171)		0.27	3.86	1.94	24 54-78
9	0.00312 (1.948)	0.00112 (2.274)	0.00102 (2.171)	-0.04600 (-5.326)	0.61	11.08	2.08	25 54-78

Note: The trade balance of Sweden is related positively to the growth rate differential. The concurrent growth rate differential and lagged terms did not contribute significantly to the regressions. The 1974 oil price shock appears to have been a major factor in the trade balance of Sweden. In Equations 8 and 9, the concurrent and leading growth rate differentials are statistically significant and positive.

121

TABLE 7A.8. Merchandise Trade Balance and Economic Growth: Switzerland

Equation	b_0	b_1	b_2	b_3	R^2	F	DW	# Observations Dates
1	0.00015 (0.048)	−0.00228 (−2.352)			0.21	5.53	1.62	23 57–79
2	−0.00070 (−0.221)	0.00265 (−2.602)			0.25	6.77	1.76	22 57–79
3	−0.00070 (−0.221)	−0.00265 (−2.602)		0.01770 (1.120)	0.26	3.43	1.72	23 57–79
4	−0.00019 (−0.065)	−0.00301 (−2.907)	−0.00165 (−1.624)		0.30	4.30	1.71	23 57–79
5	−0.00121 (−0.404)	−0.00351 (−3.259)	0.00180 (−1.801)		0.36	5.39	1.87	22 57–79
6	−0.00121 (−0.404)	−0.00351 (−3.259)	0.00180 (−1.801)	0.02070 (1.372)	0.36	3.62	1.78	23 57–79
7	0.0124 (0.396)	−0.00184 (−1.730)	0.00063 (0.591)		0.21	2.54	1.80	22 57–78
8	0.00001 (0.004)	−0.00205 (−1.977)	0.00158 (1.321)		0.30	3.92	2.26	21 57–78
9	0.00001 (0.004)	−0.00205 (−1.977)	0.00158 (1.321)	0.02768 (1.561)	0.31	2.63	2.13	22 57–78

Note: The Swiss trade balance is associated negatively with the growth rate differential. The leading terms fail to contribute significantly to the regressions, and the oil dummy is not significant in those equations. Despite the insignificant results with the dummy variable, the lagged term in Equation 5 is statistically significant when 1974 is deleted. The concurrent growth rate differential is significant and negative in all equations.

122

TABLE 7A.9. Merchandise Trade Balance and Economic Growth: United Kingdom

Equation	b_0	b_1	b_2	b_3	R^2	F	DW	# Observations Dates
1	-0.00012 (-0.034)	-0.00043 (-0.341)			0.01	0.12	1.82	19 61–79
2	0.00159 (0.524)	-0.00156 (-1.294)			0.09	1.67	2.21	18 61–79
3	0.00159 (0.524)	-0.00156 (-1.294)		-0.03516 (-2.465)	0.28	3.11	1.81	19 61–79
4	-0.00005 (-0.019)	-0.00293 (-2.331)	-0.00420 (-3.325)		0.41	5.62	1.64	19 61–79
5	0.00092 (0.345)	-0.00306 (-2.511)	-0.00333 (-2.448)		0.35	4.09	2.02	18 61–79
6	0.00092 (0.345)	-0.00306 (-2.511)	-0.00333 (-2.448)	-0.02023 (-1.459)	0.49	4.72	1.74	19 61–79
7	0.00038 (0.105)	-0.00058 (-0.344)	0.00002 (0.012)		0.01	0.10	1.81	18 61–78
8	0.00246 (0.772)	-0.00236 (-1.477)	-0.00071 (-0.494)		0.15	1.22	2.25	17 61–78
9	0.00246 (0.772)	-0.00236 (-1.477)	-0.00071 (-0.494)	-0.03886 (-2.593)	0.33	2.33	1.85	18 61–78

Note: The trade balance of the United Kingdom is related negatively to the growth rate differential. The leading terms fail to contribute statistically significant results. The concurrent terms alone do not yield significant results. Inclusion of lagged growth rate differentials yields significant coefficients for both the concurrent and lagged terms. The 1974 oil price shock does not appear to have been a major factor affecting the trade balance of the United Kingdom; the dummy variable in Equation 6 is not significant, and the R^2 of Equation 4 is slightly greater than that of Equation 5, in which 1974 is deleted.

TABLE 7A.10. Merchandise Trade Balance and Economic Growth: United States

Equation	b_0	b_1	b_2	b_3	R^2	F	DW	# Observations Dates
1	-0.00066 (-0.718)	-0.00077 (-2.409)			0.19	5.80	2.36	26 54–79
2	-0.00046 (-0.499)	-0.00080 (-2.498)			0.21	6.24	1.79	25 54–79
3	-0.00046 (-0.499)	-0.00080 (-2.498)		-0.00507 (-1.0066)	0.23	3.48	2.03	26 54–79
4	-0.00069 (-0.751)	-0.00086 (-2.587)	-0.00033 (-0.991)		0.23	3.39	2.38	26 54–79
5	-0.00047 (-0.506)	-0.00092 (-2.757)	-0.00040 (-1.189)		0.26	3.88	1.69	25 54–79
6	-0.00047 (-0.506)	-0.00092 (-2.757)	-0.00040 (-1.189)	-0.00097 (-1.251)	0.28	2.84	1.96	26 54–79
7	-0.00079 (-0.812)	-0.00073 (-2.020)	0.00007 (0.188)		0.19	2.54	2.41	25 54–78
8	-0.00059 (-0.598)	-0.00074 (-2.059)	0.00013 (0.325)		0.21	2.78	1.82	24 54–78
9	-0.00059 (-0.598)	-0.00074 (-2.059)	0.00013 (0.325)	-0.00515 (-1.034)	0.23	2.06	2.09	25 54–78

Note: The U.S. trade balance and the growth rate differential are related negatively. None of the terms incorporating lags, leads, or the oil dummy yielded statistically significant results. The concurrent growth rate differential is negative and statistically significant in all equations.

TABLE 7A.11. Merchandise Trade Balance and Economic Growth: Belgium

Equation	b_0	b_1	b_2	b_3	R^2	F	DW	# Observations Dates
1	-0.00258 (-0.883)	0.00160 (1.347)			0.11	1.81	1.59	16 64-79
2	-0.00106 (-0.385)	0.00282 (2.306)			0.29	5.32	1.76	15 64-79
3	-0.00106 (-0.385)	0.00282 (2.306)		-0.02565 (-2.053)	0.33	3.22	1.75	16 64-79
4	-0.00256 (-0.842)	0.00175 (1.243)	0.00032 (0.223)		0.12	0.87	1.61	16 64-79
5	-0.00086 (-0.305)	0.00335 (2.293)	0.00091 (0.695)		0.32	2.80	1.77	15 64-79
6	-0.00086 (-0.305)	0.00335 (2.293)	0.00091 (0.695)	-0.02759 (-2.114)	0.36	2.22	1.78	16 64-79
7	-0.00122 (-0.426)	0.00206 (1.562)	-0.00004 (-0.032)		0.21	1.63	1.46	15 64-78
8	0.00145 (0.702)	-0.00331 (3.486)	-0.00155 (-1.619)		0.64	9.73	1.90	14 64-78
9	0.00145 (0.702)	0.00331 (3.486)	-0.00155 (-1.619)	-0.03863 (-3.883)	0.67	7.39	1.86	15 64-78

Note: For Belgium the relationship between the trade balance and the growth rate differential is positive. The significance of the dummy variable indicates that the 1974 oil price shock was an important factor. Neither the lagging nor the leading coefficients contribute significantly to the regressions. The concurrent relationship is positive in all equations.

125

NOTES

1. Laffer (1977) discusses four necessary conditions for devaluation to improve the trade balance: (1) The terms of trade must deteriorate; (2) import demand responses must dominate export demand responses; (3) demand effects must dominate supply effects; (4) the Marshall–Lerner elasticity conditions must prevail.

2. The Laffer (1977) and Salant (1977) studies did not control for changes in other economic policy instruments. Marc A. Miles (1978, 1979) conducted a study measuring the effects of devaluation after considering some of these factors. The other factors included in his study were economic growth, monetary growth, and government spending. After accounting for these other factors, Miles finds no evidence of devaluation improving the trade balance. A large negative effect on the trade balance was found in the year of devaluation, and a net negative effect continued in the following three years, although a small positive effect was found in the year immediately following devaluation.

3. Since the U.S. dollar is the reference currency (arbitrarily), the dollar exchange rate will always be one, and changes will always be zero.

4. This method of computing the average tariff rate suffers from precisely the effect it is intended to illustrate, since revenues are a function of both the rate of taxation and the volume of imports. Ideally, the relevant tariff rates are those levied by government. Unfortunately, the massive tariff schedules by commodity type preclude this approach. However, one would expect that, if anything, the true tariff rates would magnify the effects shown.

5. Symmetrical results can be shown for export subsidies—that is, a subsidy to exports (negative tax) is, at the same time, a subsidy to imports.

6. The total effects on the embargo and embargoing economies as well as the effectiveness of an embargo are not intuitively obvious. For a complete discussion, see Canto and Laffer (1981).

7. The efficiency considerations mentioned here are intended to embody the notion of comparative advantage.

8. Real growth rates were computed by converting constant prices in the domestic currency GNP into constant-dollar GNP (1975 = 100). In the regression equations, the dependent variable is the change in the trade balance as a share of GNP; the explanatory variable is the growth rate differential. The basic relationship between the trade balance and economic growth is examined, incorporating leading and lagging growth rate differentials in addition to the concurrent relationship. Additionally, the trade effects of the 1974 oil price shock are considered by two alternative methods. In the first method, a dummy variable (0–1 type) is incorporated. In the second method, 1974 is deleted from the time series sample to avoid reporting inflated R^2 values resulting from the dummy variable method. (See Appendix for details.)

9. This argument encompasses traded goods, exclusive of tariffs and transportation costs. For nontraded goods whose tariffs or transportation costs are prohibitive, multiple markets may well exist. Price discrepancies across nontraded goods markets will be eliminated if factors of production are freely mobile. See Robert A. Mundell (1957).

REFERENCES

Canto, Victor A., and Arthur B. Laffer. 1981. "The Incidence of a Commodity Trade Embargo." University of Southern California. October. Unpublished.

Cooper, Richard. 1971a. "An Assessment of Currency Devaluation in Developing Countries," in G. Ranis, ed., *Government and Economic Development*. New Haven: Yale University Press.

——. 1971b. "Currency Devaluation in Developing Countries," in *Essays in International Finance, No. 86*. Princeton: Princeton University Press.

Laffer, Arthur B. 1977. "Exchange Rates, and Terms of Trade, and the Trade Balance," in Peter B. Clark, Dennis E. Logue, and Richard James Sweeney, eds., *The Effects of Exchange Rate Adjustments*. OASI Research, Department of the Treasury. Washington, D.C.: U.S. Government Printing Office, pp. 32–44.

Lerner, A. P. 1936. "The Symmetry Between Import and Export Taxes." *Economica*, Vol. 3, No. 11, August.

Miles, Marc. A. 1979. "The Effects of Devaluation on the Trade Balance and Balance of Payments: Some New Results." *Journal of Political Economy*, Vol. 87, No. 3, June.

——. 1978. *Devaluation, the Trade Balance and the Balance of Payments*. New York: Marcel Dekker.

Mundell, Robert A. 1957. "International Trade and Factor Mobility." *American Economic Review*, Vol. 47, No. 3, June, pp. 321–35.

Salant, Michael. 1977. "Devaluations Improve the Balance of Payments Even If Not the Trade Balance," in Clark et al., *Effects of Exchange Rate Adjustments*, pp. 97–114.

8
World Inflation
Arthur B. Laffer and James C. Turney

SUMMARY

The experience of the last decade proves as no other that inflation is a global phenomenon. Under the fixed exchange rate system that prevailed for a quarter-century following World War II, inflation rates among the industrial countries were moderate and closely linked. But with the collapse of the fixed exchange rate system in the early 1970s, double-digit inflation swept the global economy. With floating exchange rates, inflation as measured in local currency units diverged widely in the latter part of the decade. But when these seemingly disparate rates are expressed in a common currency unit, inflation is once again revealed as a global problem.

Money, like inflation, knows no national boundaries. The only relevant domain for money is the world itself. Since 1950 the importance of U.S. money relative to the global aggregate has declined sharply. In 1950 U.S. M1 constituted 70 percent of the world's money. By 1980 U.S. money comprised less than a quarter of the world's total. During the 1970s the monies of the rest of the world grew faster than that in the United States each and every year.

Statistical tests also point to the global money variable as having the strongest relationship with both global and U.S. inflation. When viewed in a world context, U.S. money growth is virtually irrelevant to domestic or worldwide inflation. The policy implications are far reaching:

- The current emphasis on M1 or any other U.S. monetary aggregate is misplaced.

- Higher economic growth rates contribute to lower rates of inflation.
- Ridding the United States and the world of high inflation rates must be accomplished by policies that operate within a global context.

WORLD INFLATION: THE RELEVANT DOMAIN

Long, long ago, the first U.S. monetary economist was hurriedly putting the finishing touches on his model of the Chicago economy. Gray and wrinkled, his lifetime study of the Chicago money supply, Chicago prices, and the Chicago economy was nearing completion. In room 401 in History Corner at the University of Chicago, he proudly presented his findings in a day-long seminar. The opus was well received by his colleagues.

During the entire day, a sole skeptical comment was offered. A young assistant professor from Peoria, Illinois, respectfully put forth the notion that the relevant measure of money was perhaps not confined to Chicago's city limits. This assistant professor stressed that in many visits home he was able to write checks drawn on his bank balances in Chicago. And furthermore, when he returned to Chicago, Peoria checking accounts were also quite acceptable. The young economist hypothesized that the relevant domain for a concept such as money was constrained by Illinois' borders, not Chicago's. After a brief interchange, the elder economist stroked his beard and conceded. The young economist now had his life's work placed before him.

Forty years later, long ago, the economist raised in Peoria, now gray and eyes dimmed by the passage of time, was presenting his model of the Illinois economy, The setting was reminiscent of that 40 years earlier: the same room, the same conference table, and the same chairs. The seminar went well all day. His colleagues commended him for his scholarly study of Illinois money, Illinois prices, and the Illinois economy. At the close of the seminar, once again skeptical comment was offered. A young, singularly brilliant professor from Madison, Wisconsin, offered the criticism that the relevant domain for a concept such as money was not confined to Illinois' arbitrary political boundaries. This professor's contention was that the United States' money was a more appropriate measure than Illinois' money. The elderly economist from Peoria, peering over the top of his spectacles, conceded immediately without debate. The young economist from Madison had his life's work placed before him.

A GLOBAL PERSPECTIVE

The ubiquitous nature of inflation and recession across countries in various degrees in recent years justifies labeling the phenomenon global rather than national. Economic events have been occurring in all developed nations with only minor differences (see Laffer 1975). While talk of economic "interdependence" is widespread, economic policy is still perceived as national in scope. Economic policy initiatives proceed on the premise that economies of different nations are, at best, only loosely connected.

This isolationist frame of mind has been most notable in the design of policies to control inflation. Experience, however, lends credence to the notion that domestic factors alone are not sufficient to explain domestic inflation. Moreover, policy implications that emanate from a worldwide view of inflation are very different from those resulting from a closed economy perspective.

Whether true or not, one can imagine that the monetary authorities could control a closed economy's money supply—say, demand deposits plus currency. In the world economy, however, control, as a practical matter, borders on inconceivable. The role of any one country's monetary authority—such as the U.S. Federal Reserve Board—wanes dramatically in the perspective of the world.

Money is, after all, one of the easiest commodities to move across national borders. Individual banks and other financial institutions operate in numerous U.S. and foreign locations. Even when the foreign operations are not direct subsidiaries, correspondent relationships and other close associations have been developed. Money markets not only within the United States but also in the world economy are closely interrelated by this vast financial network (see Cooper 1968, 1969; Roper 1971; Evans and Laffer 1977; Miles 1978; Agman 1980; Griton and Roper 1981; Canto and Miles 1983). The advent of floating exchange rates has not led to the dissolution of integrated money markets. With spot and forward foreign exchange markets, floating rates, at most, have added only somewhat to the cost of operating in those markets (see Friedman and Schwartz 1963, 1970).

Considerable disagreement exists as to what are the relevant quantities of money and goods that determine the inflation rate in a given locality or country. The local view argues that the relevant concepts of money and output are the national (local) quantities. The global view argues that the relevant concepts of money and output in their relationship with inflation are the world quantities.

This essay presents a "global monetarist" view of inflation and money. It incorporates into the analysis a worldwide integration of money and product markets. In contrast to the local monetarist view, U.S. money and U.S. production are considered to be only a fraction of their global counterparts. Global money and global production are the relevant dimensions for examining inflation, be it global inflation or inflation in a specific country such as the United States.

INFLATION

Inflation is a worldwide phenomenon, affecting all developed nations simultaneously. In general, prices are arbitraged internationally. A vast array of products as well as factors of production move easily across national borders. Viewing the world as a single economic unit, the global rate of inflation assumes a unique role of importance.

Global inflation could be expressed in any single numeraire. This study measures inflation in U.S. dollar terms. World inflation in dollars can be measured in any number of ways [for example, using a weighted average of individual country consumer price indexes or wholesale price indexes (WPIs) converted to dollars]. The method chosen for this study is equivalent to a world gross national product (GNP) price deflator.[1]

Global inflation was moderate in the 1950s and 1960s compared with the 1970s. The average annual inflation rate was 2.3 percent in the decade of the 1950s, 2.7 percent in the 1960s, and 9.1 percent in the 1970s (Graph 8.1).

Two notable features of changes in the world price level, revealed by Graph 8.1, are (1) world inflation begins an increasing trend in 1968 or 1969, and (2) during the 1970s the year-to-year swings in the world inflation rate become larger. In previous years, the rate of inflation was low and relatively stable.

The change in the pattern exhibited by global inflation coincides directly with the end to U.S. dollar/gold convertibility embodied by the Bretton Woods monetary system (see Turney 1980). Since the end of dollar convertibility (March 1968 with private parties and August 1971 with official parties), world inflation has been rising—both its level and volatility.

Integration of the world market implies that domestic price levels in each and every specific country reflect in part the world price level. Furthermore, changes in domestic price levels reflect the global rate of inflation. Domestic inflation, measured by prices denominated in any spe-

GRAPH 8.1. Global Inflation Expressed in U.S. Dollars, 1950–79

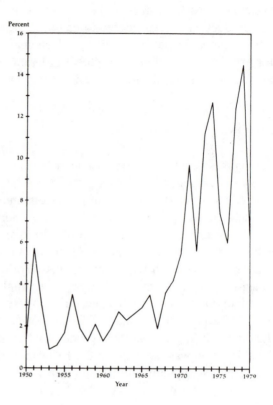

End-of-year data.

Sources: BIS Annual Report, Bank for International Settlements, Basel, Switzerland. *OECD National Accounts,* Department of Economics and Statistics, Organization for Economic Co-operation and Development, Paris. *International Financial Statistics,* Bureau of Statistics, International Monetary Fund, Washington, D.C.

cific local currency (for example, inflation in France measured by changes in franc prices), will also reflect changes in the value of the currency, that is, the exchange rate (Laffer and Turney 1982).

During the entire post-World War II era, inflation in the United States has been roughly equal to world inflation expressed in dollars (Figure 8.1). The correlation coefficient between the annual rates is high—0.79. For the most part, changes in U.S. prices mirror changes in the world price level.

FIGURE 8.1.   U.S. Inflation and World Inflation,[a] 1950–79

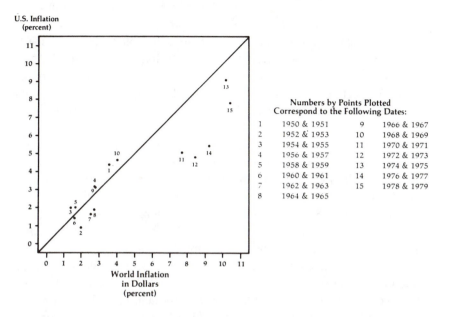

U.S. Inflation
(percent)

Numbers by Points Plotted
Correspond to the Following Dates:

1	1950 & 1951	9	1966 & 1967
2	1952 & 1953	10	1968 & 1969
3	1954 & 1955	11	1970 & 1971
4	1956 & 1957	12	1972 & 1973
5	1958 & 1959	13	1974 & 1975
6	1960 & 1961	14	1976 & 1977
7	1962 & 1963	15	1978 & 1979
8	1964 & 1965		

World Inflation
in Dollars
(percent)

[a]Biennial rates of inflation expressed in U.S. dollar terms.

Sources: BIS Annual Report, Bank for International Settlements, Basel, Switzerland. *OECD National Accounts,* Department of Economics and Statistics, Organization for Economic Co-operation and Development, Paris. *International Financial Statistics,* Bureau of Statistics, International Monetary Fund, Washington, D.C.

SOURCES OF WORLD MONEY

Money knows no national boundaries. To money, the political sub-divisions of the world are little different from the Chicago city limits or the Illinois state line. The only relevant domain for money is the world itself. While the debate over which aggregate corresponds to domestic money is likely to continue, the measure of domestic money selected for this essay is "money" as reported in *International Financial Statistics,* published by the International Monetary Fund, Washington, D.C. This measure of money corresponds closely to M1 while allowing for differences among countries.

For analytic purposes, each domestic component of world money must be expressed in a single numeraire in order to permit aggregation. Just as the world production of oil could be expressed in U.S. gallons or liters, barrels also provide a common unit of measure. The U.S. dollar has been chosen as the unit of measure of world money.[2]

The measure of world money used here is the dollar value of domestic monies of 11 major countries plus net Eurodollar deposits.[3] U.S. M1 is expressed in dollars. The M1 values of the rest of the world are reported in their respective domestic currency units. These quantities then are converted into dollar amounts using the appropriate prevailing dollar exchange rates.

World money, inclusive of Eurodollars, in dollars increased by nearly 12-fold during the 31 years ending in 1979. That is an annual average rate of growth of 8.2 percent. In 1949 world money is estimated to have been $154 billion. By 1960 world money totaled $244 billion and more than doubled to $533 billion in 1970. This measure of world money sailed through the $1 trillion mark during 1975. By the end of 1980 the dollar value of world money reached $2 trillion (Graph 8.2).

The most striking feature of the sources of world money is the decline in the importance of U.S. money. In 1950 U.S. money constituted 70 percent of the world supply. By 1966 less than half of world money was located in the United States. In 1979 U.S. money composed only 22 percent of the total (Graph 8.2).

The annual growth rates of world money exhibit an increasing trend starting in the late 1950s. During the early 1960s world money growth remained relatively steady. But beginning in the late 1960s or early 1970s, a virtual explosion of world money occurred, the rate of expansion declining somewhat during the middle 1970s. In 1978 world money grew at a 21.7 annual rate, falling back to an 8.2 percent growth rate in 1979. Comparing the decades, world money growth averaged 2 percent per annum during the 1950s, 7.2 percent during the 1960s, and 13.3 percent in the 1970s.

The growth rate of world money can be partitioned into U.S. money growth, other domestic money growth valued in domestic currency, currency exchange rate changes, and Eurodollar growth.

The punctuated line in Graph 8.3 represents the effect on world money growth of U.S. money alone. Adding to that the effect of other countries' domestic monies provides the dashed line. The dotted line adds in the effect of exchange rate changes on world money growth. Finally, the solid line adds in the effect of Eurodollars to show the total growth rate of world money from 1950 to 1979.

**GRAPH 8.2. World Money in U.S. Dollars
and Its Components, 1949–79**

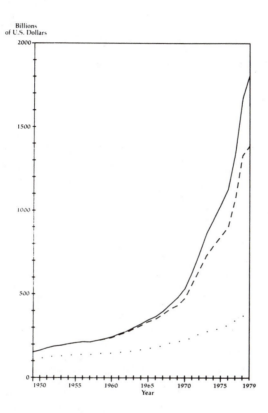

End-of-year data.
——— World money: Eurodollars, plus rest-of-world M1 in dollars, plus U.S. M1.
– – – – – Rest-of-world M1 (ten countries) stated in U.S. dollars, plus U.S. M1.
. . . . . . U.S. M1.

Sources: BIS Annual Report, Bank for International Settlements, Basel, Switzerland. *OECD National Accounts,* Department of Economics and Statistics, Organization for Economic Co-operation and Development, Paris. *International Financial Statistics,* Bureau of Statistics, International Monetary Fund, Washington, D.C.

U.S. Money Growth

The contribution of U.S. money to the growth rate in world money diminishes during the 30-year period. A comparison of the average an-

GRAPH 8.3. Sources of World Money Growth, 1950–79

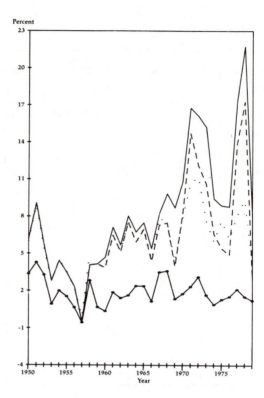

End-of-year data.
■──■──■ U.S. M1.
------ Plus ten other countries' M1, expressed in domestic currency.
. . . . . . Plus ten currency exchange rates with the U.S. dollar.
──────── Plus Eurodollars.

Sources: BIS Annual Report, Bank for International Settlements, Basel, Switzerland. *OECD National Accounts,* Department of Economics and Statistics, Organization for Economic Co-operation and Development, Paris. *International Financial Statistics,* Bureau of Statistics, International Monetary Fund, Washington, D.C.

nual growth rates of each component of world money growth during the decades of the 1950s, 1960s, and 1970s is provided in Table 8.1

U.S. money growth constitutes less than half of total world money growth in each and every decade. U.S. money growth is not the most important source of world money growth in any decade examined. Over the three decades, the importance of U.S. money as a source of world money growth declines sharply relative to the other sources.

Rest-of-World Domestic Money

The domestic monies of the rest of the world are by far the most important source of world money growth, and increasingly so as the decades pass. Although the rest of the world contributed only slightly more to world money growth than the United States in the 1950s, other domestic monies contributed twice as much as the United States in the 1960s and more than three times as much in the 1970s (Table 8.1).

TABLE 8.1. Sources of World Money Growth
(Annual Percentage Changes Weighted by Contribution)

| Year | Domestic Money | | Exchange Rates | Eurodollars | Total World Money |
	United States	Rest of World			
1950–59 Average	1.9	2.4	−0.1 (0.3)	—	4.2
1960–69 Average	1.9	4.1	−0.1 (0.2)	1.3	7.2
1970–79 Average	1.7	6.2	1.8 (2.7)	3.6	13.3
1970	1.8	6.1	0.3	2.6	10.8
1971	2.3	8.4	4.0	2.1	16.8
1972	3.1	8.1	0.9	4.0	16.1
1973	1.6	6.0	3.0	4.6	15.2
1974	0.9	5.1	0.6	2.8	9.4
1975	1.3	6.4	−2.2	3.4	8.9
1976	1.5	4.7	−1.3	3.9	8.8
1977	2.1	5.9	5.8	3.5	17.3
1978	1.5	7.8	7.9	4.5	21.7
1979	1.2	3.1	−1.2	5.1	8.2

Notes: End-of-year data.

Parentheses indicate absolute percentage changes. These statistics are shown in addition to the nominal percentage changes to avoid concealing the importance of exchange rate effects by nominal averaging. With nominal averaging, negative changes cancel positive changes. Negative growth rates affect the other averages shown only trivially.

Sources: BIS Annual Report, Bank for International Settlements, Basel, Switzerland. *International Financial Statistics,* Bureau of Statistics, International Monetary Fund, Washington, D.C.

Effect of Exchange Rate Changes on World Money

The currency exchange rate effect depends solely on the specific currency selected as numeraire for world money. To illustrate, imagine that there are 200 Deutsche marks and the exchange rate is four marks per U.S. dollar. The dollar value of German money is $50. Suppose the dollar devalues to a new exchange rate of two marks to the dollar. The dollar value of the 200 marks is now $100. Thus, even though the quantity of marks is stable, German money contributes twice as much to the stock of world money measured in dollars following depreciation of the dollar. Depreciation of the dollar relative to other currencies implies an increase in the dollar-denominated world money aggregate. Conversely, if a different numeraire had been selected, dollar devaluation implies a reduction in the foreign currency value of world money. If measured in a generally appreciating currency, say, the Swiss franc, world money growth would be slower.

Exchange rate changes had a minor effect on world money growth in the 1950s and 1960s when the Bretton Woods fixed exchange rates were in force. During these two decades, the average effect of exchange rates was a slight reduction in the growth rate of world money. The absolute effect shown in parentheses is also insignificantly small (Table 8.1). But during the 1970s exchange rates were an important component of world money growth, exceeding the effect of U.S. money growth. Exchange rate changes contributed both positively and negatively to world money growth in recent years. The average effect of exchange rate changes during the 1970s was to increase the growth rate of world money measured in U.S. dollars.

Eurodollars

Eurodollars play a somewhat special role in the world financial system.

1. To the extent that Eurodollars pay a competitive interest rate, they are indexed and do not suffer an inflation tax. As inflation increases, holders of money balances will tend to shift their balances toward this kind of money. Evidence of this substitution is presented in Graph 8.4. The secular increase in the inflation rate, holding everything else the same, will induce money holders to substitute away from non-interest-bearing currency and demand deposits into interest-bearing forms of money such as Eurodollars and money market funds. This substitution effect will lead

to a secular increase in the velocity of the non-interest-bearing money. The substitution effect away from M1 to other forms of money will tend to leave unchanged the overall quantity of broadly defined money and thus velocity. In fact, since 1950 the velocity of U.S. M1 and world M1 has increased while the velocity of world money including Eurodollars has remained relatively constant.

2. Other interesting aspects of Eurodollars are that Eurodollars may partially offset changes in domestic money growth—thus making the quan-

GRAPH 8.4. The Effect of Eurodollars on Velocity and World Money Growth

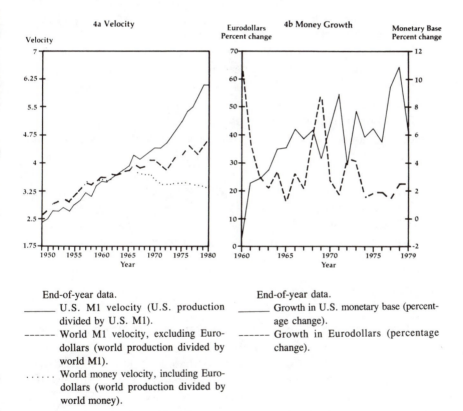

End-of-year data.

_____ U.S. M1 velocity (U.S. production divided by U.S. M1).

------ World M1 velocity, excluding Eurodollars (world production divided by world M1).

...... World money velocity, including Eurodollars (world production divided by world money).

End-of-year data.

_____ Growth in U.S. monetary base (percentage change).

------ Growth in Eurodollars (percentage change).

Sources: BIS Annual Report, Bank for International Settlements, Basel, Switzerland. *OECD National Accounts,* Department of Economics and Statistics, Organization for Economic Co-operation and Development, Paris. *International Financial Statistics,* Bureau of Statistics, International Monetary Fund, Washington, D.C.

tity of money partially endogenous. The negative relationship between growth in the U.S. monetary base and growth in Eurodollars since 1960 indicates that the Eurodollar market has provided a partial offset to U.S. domestic monetary policy (Graph 8.4b).

Eurocurrencies do represent a viable substitute for domestic monies. Suppliers (banks) often have a choice of producing local currency-denominated balances or participating in non-local currency deposit taking and lending. Likewise, demanders (depositors) can often choose deposits in the country of origin or in the Eurocurrency market. Profit considerations imply that as the costs of local currency balances rise, Eurocurrency alternatives become more attractive.

The ability of Eurocurrencies to substitute for domestic deposits implies that monetary policy initiatives by domestic authorities are potentially offset. Changes in reserve requirements, the discount rate, and open market operations affect the costs of the domestic banking system, while the Eurocurrency system is relatively free from those regulations.[4] If a monetary authority implements policies that would have the effect of contracting domestic money, the Eurocurrency market becomes relatively less costly and can expand to absorb the excess demand for money.

The Eurodollar market emerged in the 1960s with a minor impact on world money. However, during the decade of the 1970s, Eurodollars were the second most important source of world money growth, accounting for more than twice the contribution of U.S. money. In 1979 Eurodollars were the largest component of world money growth. In fact, the size of the Eurodollar market surpassed that of U.S. money in 1979. Eurodollars in 1980 amounted to $538 billion, 27 percent of world money, while U.S. M1 totaled $424 billion, 21 percent of world money.

SOURCES OF GLOBAL INFLATION

Money is not the exclusive source of changes in the world price level. In addition to growth in the quantity of world money, the growth in the quantity of world production is related to inflation. Inflation is frequently defined as too much money chasing too few goods. That is, all else the same, an increase in the growth rate of money is associated with a higher inflation rate. Similarly, an increase in the growth rate of output reduces the rate of inflation. From a global monetarist perspective, the relevant quantities of money and output are the world measures. Increases in the growth rate of world money raise global inflation. Declining production growth raises the rate of global inflation.

The growth rate of world production adjusted for inflation is divided into two components: growth attributable to U.S. production and that attributable to the rest-of-world production (Graph 8.5). Total world production grew at a 4.6 percent average rate during the 1950s. It went up to 5.1 percent in the 1960s, and slowed down to 3.5 percent in the 1970s. The U.S. contribution to world production was 1.8 percent during the 1950s, 2.1 percent in the 1960s, and 1.4 percent in the 1970s. The U.S. share of total world production was relatively constant over the entire period (Table 8.2).

Global inflation can be partitioned into the component due to money growth and the component due to output growth. In Graph 8.6 the inflationary impact of world production growth is shown by the dotted line. Adding vertically to the dotted line is the inflationary impact of world money growth, yielding the dashed line.

A surprising characteristic of the sources of global inflation is that no single component dominates as "most important" during all three decades (Table 8.3). During the 1950s the growth rate of world production was the most important component, tending to reduce global inflation, while world money growth contributed moderately to inflation.

World money growth emerged as the largest component of global inflation in the 1960s. Production growth again reduced global inflation and by a significant amount.

The growth of world money continued to dominate as the most important source of global inflation in the 1970s. World production growth was sharply lower in the 1970s than in earlier decades, offering a smaller effect in reducing the global rate of inflation. The dramatic increase in global inflation during the 1970s was largely attributable to the surge in world money growth and sharp decline in world production growth.

THE GLOBAL SOLUTION

A statistical analysis relating the importance of changes in the U.S. output, U.S. money, rest-of-world output, and rest-of-world money to the U.S. inflation rate points to the primacy of the global variables in understanding the phenomenon of inflation.

The local and global monetarist models of inflation are juxtaposed in Table 8.4. The regression equations examine both local inflation in the United States [as measured by the U.S. gross domestic product (GDP) price deflator] and global inflation (as measured by the world GDP price deflator, expressed in U.S. dollar terms).

GRAPH 8.5. World Production in U.S. Dollars, 1951–79

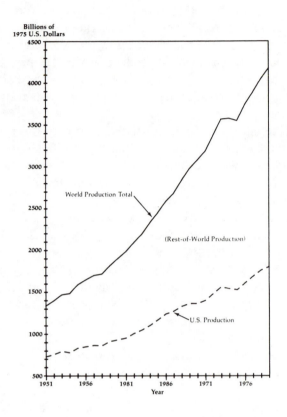

End-of-year data.

_____ World production.

------ U.S. production.

Sources: BIS Annual Report, Bank for International Settlements, Basel, Switzerland. *OECD National Accounts,* Department of Economics and Statistics, Organization for Economic Co-operation and Development, Paris. *International Financial Statistics,* Bureau of Statistics, International Monetary Fund, Washington, D.C.

The local monetarist version of U.S. inflation is confirmed by Equation 1. The coefficients are of the expected sign (money growth is positive and production growth negative) and the t statistics significant. The explanatory power of regression is impressive with $R^2 = 0.52$ and the F statistic significant.

**TABLE 8.2.   Sources of World Production Growth
(Annual Percentage Change)**

Year	U.S. Contribution to World Production[a]	Rest-of-World Contribution to World Production	Total World Production
1950–59 Average	1.8	2.7	4.5
1960–69 Average	1.9	3.0	4.9
1970–79 Average	1.2	2.2	3.4
1970	−0.1	3.4	3.3
1971	1.3	2.2	3.5
1972	2.5	2.8	5.3
1973	2.3	3.7	6.0
1974	−0.5	0.8	0.3
1975	−0.4	−0.3	−0.7
1976	2.3	3.0	5.3
1977	2.0	1.8	3.8
1978	1.9	2.1	4.0
1979	1.0	2.2	3.2

[a]U.S. production growth=[log (U.S. production (t)/U.S. production $(t-1)$)]·(U.S. production (t)/world production (t)).

Sources: BIS Annual Report, Bank for International Settlements, Basel, Switzerland. *International Financial Statistics,* Bureau of Statistics, International Monetary Fund, Washington, D.C.

The global monetarist version of U.S. inflation is also confirmed by the data. In Equation 2, the coefficients are in the expected direction with significant t statistics. The explanatory power of the global model is even more impressive than the local model with $R^2 = 0.71$ and a significant F statistic.

The relationship between global inflation and the U.S. variables (Equation 4) is quite similar to the U.S. inflation regression (Equation 1). The $R^2 = 0.48$ reveals a strong association with a significant F statistic. The coefficients are in the expected direction and statistically significant.

The regression of global inflation on global money and global production (Equation 5) is also similar to the U.S. inflation regression (Equation 2). The $R^2 = 0.77$ is quite high and the F statistic is significant. The coefficients are in the expected direction and significant.

These results provide a strong indication that the explanatory power of the global variables is superior to that of the local (U.S.) variables in

GRAPH 8.6. Sources of Global Inflation, 1950–79

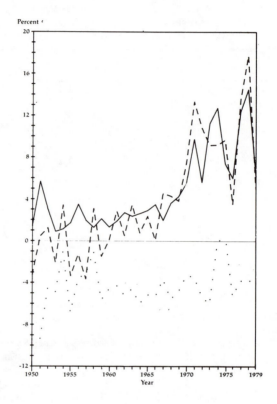

End-of-year data.

———— Global inflation: world money growth plus percentage change in world money velocity.
------ World money growth less world real production growth.
. . . . . . World real production growth, negative in sign to illustrate the inflationary impact of growth.

Sources: BIS Annual Report, Bank for International Settlements, Basel, Switzerland. *OECD National Accounts,* Department of Economics and Statistics, Organization for Economic Co-operation and Development, Paris. *International Financial Statistics,* Bureau of Statistics, International Monetary Fund, Washington, D.C.

their relationship with both local inflation and global inflation. Whether or not the addition of the local variables to the global variables contributes significantly to the regression equations is tested using Equations 3 and 6. The local monetarist variables do not contribute significantly to the global monetarist version of either U.S. inflation or global inflation. The global monetarist variables, on the other hand, add significantly to

TABLE 8.3. Sources of Global Inflation (Annual Percentage Changes)

Year	World Money	World Production[a]	Total Inflation[b]
1950–59 Average	4.2	−5.0	2.3
1960–69 Average	7.2	−4.9	2.7
1970–79 Average	13.3	−3.4	9.1
1970	10.8	−3.3	5.5
1971	16.8	−3.5	9.7
1972	16.1	−5.3	5.6
1973	15.2	−6.1	11.2
1974	9.4	−0.3	12.7
1975	8.9	0.7	7.4
1976	8.8	−5.3	6.0
1977	17.3	−3.8	12.4
1978	21.8	−4.0	14.5
1979	8.2	−3.2	6.2

[a]Increasing production growth is shown with a negative sign to illustrate the inflationary effect of this component.

[b]The sum of world money growth and world production does not add to world inflation because of changes in velocity.

Sources: BIS Annual Report, Bank for International Settlements, Basel, Switzerland. *OECD National Accounts,* Department of Economics and Statistics, Organization for Economic Co-operation and Development, Paris. *International Financial Statistics,* Bureau of Statistics, International Monetary Fund, Washington, D.C.

the explanatory power of the relation for both local inflation and global inflation.[5]

Several conclusions and one nonconclusion can be drawn from the statistical results presented in Table 8.4:

1. The local monetarist model of local inflation cannot be rejected.
2. The global monetarist model of local inflation and the global monetarist model of global inflation cannot be rejected either.
3. The explanatory power of the global monetarist model is greater than that of the local monetarist model for both U.S. inflation and global inflation.[6]
4. Addition of the local monetarist variables fails to improve upon the global monetarist model of both U.S. inflation and global inflation.
5. The equations of Table 8.4 demonstrate only association between variables; no tests of causality are conducted.

TABLE 8.4. Inflation, Money Growth, and Economic Growth, 1952–79

	R^2	F	DW	(SE)
	Residual Autocorrelation 1	2	3	

U.S. Inflation

(1) $P_{US}=2.18+0.80m_{US}-0.54g_{US}+e$
    (2.79)(4.72) (−3.69)

| | 0.52 | 13.63 | 1.14 | |
| | 0.33 | 0.23 | 0.02 | (0.19) |

(2) $P_{US}=3.44+0.37mw-0.67gw+e$
    (4.37)(6.52) (−4.59)

| | 0.71 | 30.94 | 1.45 | |
| | 0.20 | 0.03 | −0.25 | (0.19) |

(3) $P_{US}=3.71+0.03m_{US}+0.12g_{US}+0.35mw-0.82gw+e$
    (3.67)(0.10) (0.46) (2.88) (−2.36)

| | 0.72 | 14.45 | 1.45 | |
| | 0.20 | −0.02 | −0.27 | (0.19) |

Global Inflation

(4) $P_W=0.62+1.35m_{US}-0.43g_{US}+e$
    (0.47)(4.76) (−1.78)

| | 0.48 | 11.33 | 1.27 | |
| | 0.33 | 0.07 | 0.20 | (0.19) |

(5) $P_W=1.07+0.71mw-0.53gw+e$
    (0.96)(8.98) (−2.58)

| | 0.77 | 42.96 | 1.74 | |
| | 0.06 | −0.17 | 0.14 | (0.19) |

(6) $P_W = 2.44 - 0.50 m_{US} + 0.60 g_{US} + 0.86 m_W - 1.15 g_W + e$
    $\quad\ (1.86)(-1.37)\quad (1.75)\quad\ (5.48)\quad (-2.54)$

0.81	24.39	1.81
0.03	−0.32	0.14	(0.19)

Notes: t statistics in parentheses; DW, Durbin–Watson statistic; annual data; data for money growth use midpoint averages computed using end-of-year observations.

Sources: BIS Annual Report, Bank for International Settlements, Basel, Switzerland. *OECD National Accounts*, Department of Economics and Statistics, Organization for Economic Co-operation and Development, Paris. *International Financial Statistics*, Bureau of Statistics, International Monetary Fund, Washington, D.C.

Variable definitions:

P_{US} = U.S. inflation rate, annually, computed as the percentage change in the U.S. GDP price deflator
P_W = World inflation rate, annually, computed as the percentage change in aggregate dollar world GDP price deflator
m_{US} = U.S. money growth rate, annually, computed as the percentage change in U.S. M1
m_W = World money growth rate, annually, computed as the percentage change in total world money expressed in U.S. dollars
g_{US} = U.S. production growth rate in real terms, annually, computed as the percentage change in constant-dollar U.S. GDP
g_W = World production growth rate in real terms, annually, computed as the percentage change in constant-dollar aggregate world GDP.
e = residual

147

The equations in Table 8.5 extend the global model of U.S. and world inflation by partitioning global money and production into U.S. and non-U.S. components.

Once again, the results are striking. In Equation 1, the coefficients are all of the expected sign; that is, increases in the growth rate of the monetary aggregates are associated with increases in the inflation rate. Increases in the output components are negatively related to inflation.

Allowing U.S. money to compete statistically with rest-of-world money, however, reveals that the dominant association between the monetary aggregates and inflation is the rest-of-world money and U.S. inflation. The statistical contribution of U.S. money to U.S. inflation is not significantly different from zero. Both U.S. and rest-of-world production growth rates make a statistically significant contribution to the regression.

The results in Equation 2 with global inflation are similar to those in Equation 1. Once again, U.S. money does not make a significant contribution to world inflation, while the contribution of rest-of-world money to world inflation is statistically significant. The coefficients of the production growth variables parallel the results for money growth. U.S. economic growth does not appear significant in its contribution to global inflation. Rest-of-world economic growth, however, is significant. Both variables have the expected sign.

The single clearest and most consistent result provided by Table 8.5 is that U.S. money growth is virtually irrelevant to inflation, be it U.S. or global inflation. In both equations non-U.S. money is associated with inflation.

CONCLUSIONS

In view of this evidence, narrowly conceived policy to control the U.S. money supply is unjustified. From the standpoint of the world economy, the United States has little effect on the rate of monetary expansion and thus the world inflation rate. Foreign monies and changes in the dollar value of foreign currencies are far more important to the growth of world money than actions of the Federal Reserve, even if the Fed could control the quantity of U.S. money (see Laffer and Miles 1977a, b, 1978).

The policy implications are far reaching:

- The current emphasis on M1 or any other U.S. monetary aggregate is misplaced. To the extent that U.S. monetary authorities base their policies on the quantity of money, the focus should be on the

TABLE 8.5. Inflation and the Components of World Money Growth and World Economic Growth, 1952–79

	R^2	F	DW	Residual Autocorrelation			(SE)
				1	2	3	
(1) $P_{US}=4.16+0.06m_{US}{\cdot}SWM1_{US}+0.40m_R{\cdot}SWM1_R-0.59g_{US}{\cdot}SWY_{US}-0.70g_R{\cdot}SWY_R+e$ (3.70)(0.13) (4.43) (−1.88) (−1.75)	0.63	9.87	1.29	0.30	0.05	−0.11	(0.19)
(2) $P_W=2.48+0.09\,m_{US}{\cdot}SWM1_{US}+0.83m_R{\cdot}SWM1_R-0.19g_{US}{\cdot}SWY_{US}-0.82g_R{\cdot}SWY_R+e$ (1.77)(0.17) (7.39) (−0.49) (−1.64)	0.77	19.48	1.66	0.12	−0.27	0.12	(0.19)

Notes: t statistics in parentheses; DW, Durbin–Watson statistic; annual data; data for money growth use midpoint averages computed using end-of-year observations.

Sources: BIS Annual Report, Bank for International Settlements, Basel, Switzerland. *OECD National Accounts*, Department of Economics and Statistics, Organization for Economic Co-operation and Development, Paris. *International Financial Statistics*, Bureau of Statistics, International Monetary Fund, Washington, D.C.

Variable definitions:

P_{US}	= U.S. inflation rate, annually, computed as the percentage change in the U.S. GDP deflator
P_W	= World inflation rate, annually, computed as the percentage change in aggregate dollar world GDP price deflator
m_{US}	= U.S. money growth rate, annually, computed as the percentage change in U.S. M1
m_R	= Rest-of-world money growth rate, annually, computed as the percentage change in aggregate M1 of the rest of world, expressed in U.S. dollars
g_{US}	= U.S. production growth rate in real terms, annually, computed as the percentage change in constant-dollar U.S. GDP
g_R	= Rest-of-world production growth rate in real terms, annually, computed as the percentage change in aggregate constant-dollar GDP of the rest of the world
$SWM1_{US}$	= U.S. share of world M1, annually, computed as U.S. M1 divided by aggregate world M1, expressed in U.S. dollars
$SWM1_R$	= Rest-of-world share of world M1, annually, computed as aggregate rest-of-world M1 divided by aggregate world M1, expressed in U.S. dollars
SWY_{US}	= U.S. share of world production, annually, computed as U.S. constant-dollar GDP divided by aggregate world constant-dollar GDP
SWY_R	= Rest-of-world share of world production, annually, computed as aggregate rest-of-world constant-dollar GDP divided by world constant-dollar GDP.
e	= residual

149

150 / Monetary Policy

worldwide counterpart of M1. For example, the 20 percent appreciation of the dollar in foreign exchange markets in the 12 months ending May 1982 indicates that the growth rate of the world money supply expressed in dollars has declined relative to the growth in worldwide production. This is consistent with the sharp decline in the U.S. inflation rate in the 12 months ending May 1982.

• The analysis provides important evidence that, holding monetary policy constant, higher economic growth rates contribute to lower inflation rates. Thus, a fiscal policy aimed at augmenting output and employment is consistent with a slowdown in inflation.

• Resolution of the inflation problem that has plagued the United States and world economies for the last decade must be accomplished in a global context.

NOTES

1. The data used were actually GDP rather than GNP. The technical difference is that GDP excludes net factor income from abroad. The quantitative difference between GDP and GNP is slight.

2. The value of the dollar, of course, is not currently fixed over time as is the exchange ratio of gallons to liters or gallons to barrels.

3. The 11 countries included in this study are Belgium, Canada, France, Germany, Italy, Japan, the Netherlands, Sweden, Switzerland, the United Kingdom, and the United States. Eurodollar data encompass only the eight European countries reporting to the Bank for International Settlements (BIS), Basel, Switzerland, excluding Canada and Japan from the aforementioned.

4. Reserve requirements and the discount rate are nothing more than a tax on domestic banking activity (see Kadlec and Laffer 1979).

5. Using Equation 3 in conjunction with Equation 2 (Table 8.4), the local variables fail to contribute statistically to the explanation of U.S. inflation when added to the global variables ($F = 0.12$). Using Equation 6 in conjunction with Equation 5, U.S. money and U.S. production growth also fail to add information in the global inflation regression ($F = 2.09$). Using Equation 3 in conjunction with Equation 1, the R^2 value improves significantly when global money and global production are included in the U.S. inflation regression ($F = 7.82$). The global variables add significantly to the local variables in the explanatory power of the global inflation regression, using Equations 6 and 4 ($F = 20.11$). For further information, see Turney (1982).

6. This possibility was examined by constructing a weighted sum of domestic money growth rate and Eurodollar growth without using the exchange rate. These results are difficult to interpret because there is no single numeraire. However, the regression analyses using variables constructed in this way support the results reported in this essay (see Turney 1982).

REFERENCES

Agman, Tamir. 1980. "International Money in a Multiple Currency World: The Internationalization of the Yen." Unpublished manuscript, University of Southern California, November.

Canto, Victor A., and Marc A. Miles. 1983. "Exchange Rates in a Global Monetary Model with Currency Substitutions and Rational Expectations." In *Economic Interdependence and Flexible Exchange Rates,* edited by J. Bhandari and B. Putnam. Cambridge, MA: MIT Press, pp. 157-176.

Cooper, Richard N. 1969. "Macroeconomic Policy Adjustment in Interdependent Economies." *Quarterly Journal of Economics,* Vol. 83, No. 1, February.

———. 1968. *The Economics of Interdependence.* New York: McGraw-Hill.

Evans, Paul, and Arthur B. Laffer, 1977. "Demand Substitutability across Currencies." Unpublished manuscript, Stanford University and University of Southern California.

Friedman, Milton, and Anna Jacobson Schwartz. 1970. *Monetary Statistics of the United States.* National Bureau of Economic Research, Cambridge, MA.

———. 1963. *A Monetary History of the United States, 1867-1960.* Princeton: Princeton University Press.

Griton, Lance, and Don Roper. 1981. "Theory and Implications of Currency Substitution." *Journal of Money, Credit, and Banking,* Vol. 12, No. 1, February.

International Monetary Fund. *International Financial Statistics.* Washington, DC: Bureau of Statistics, International Monetary Fund.

Kadlec, Charles W., and Arthur B. Laffer. 1979. "The Monetary Crisis: A Classical Perspective." Economic Study, A.B. Laffer Associates, Lomita, CA, November 12.

Laffer, Arthur B. 1975. "The Phenomenon of Worldwide Inflation: A Study in Market Integration." In *The Phenomenon of World Inflation,* edited by Arthur B. Laffer and David Meiselman. Washington, D.C.: American Enterprise Institute, pp.27-53.

Laffer, Arthur B., and Marc A. Miles. 1978. "Distortions in the Seasonal Adjustments of the Official Money Supply Data." Economic Study, H. C. Wainwright & Co. Economics, September 20.

———. 1977a. "Factors Influencing Changes in the Money Supply over the Short-Term." Economic Study, H. C. Wainwright & Co. Economics, Boston, MA. August 18.

———. 1977b. "Constraints on the Usefulness of Just-Released Money Supply Figures." Economic Study, H. C. Wainwright & Co. Economics, Boston, MA. December 13.

Laffer, Arthur B., and James C. Turney. 1982. "Trade Policy and the U.S. Economy." Economic Study, A.B. Laffer Associates, Lomita, CA, March 24.

Miles, Marc A. 1978. "Currency Substitution, Flexible Exchange Rates, and Monetary Independence." *American Economic Review,* Vol. 68, No. 3, June.

Roper, Don E. 1971. "Macroeconomic Policies and the Distribution of the World Money Supply." *Quarterly Journal of Finance,* Vol. 85, No. 1, February.

Turney, James C. 1982. "Essays in International Economics." Dissertation submitted to Graduate School of Business Administration, University of Southern California, March 5.

———. 1980. "Gold." Economic Study, A.B. Laffer Associates, Lomita, CA, January 25.

Index

About the Editors

Victor A. Canto

Dr. Canto received a B.Sc. from the Massachusetts Institute of Technology and a M.A. and Ph.D in Economics from the University of Chicago. He is Senior Vice-President of A.B. Laffer Associates. He has been an Assistant Professor and an Associate Professor at the University of Southern California as well as a Visiting Professor at the Universidad Central Del Este, Dominican Republic.

In addition to his academic positions, Dr. Canto has been Economics Advisor to the Finance Minister of the Dominican Republic, Economist for the Economics Studies Division of the Dominican Republic Central Bank, as well as a consultant to Puerto Rico's Treasury and Government Financial Council.

Dr. Canto's other books include *The Financial Analyst's Guide to Fiscal Policy, Foundations of Supply Side Economics, Apuntaciones Sobre Inflación y Economía en República Dominicana,* and *The Determinants and Consequences of Trade Restrictions on the U.S. Economy.* His publications have appeared in *Economic Inquiry, Southern Economic Journal, Public Finance, Journal of International Money and Finance,* and *Journal of Macroeconomics,* among others.

Charles W. Kadlec

Charles W. Kadlec is Executive Vice-President and Director of Research of A. B. Laffer Associates. Mr. Kadlec obtained his M.B.A. with honors at the University of Chicago. His area of interest was international trade and finance. Prior to that time, he was a member of the *Business Week* editorial staff. Before joining A. B. Laffer Associates, Mr. Kadlec worked in the international division of Crocker Bank in San Francisco, and was a general partner of H. C. Wainwright & Co. Economics, Boston.

Mr. Kadlec is the coauthor of *The Financial Analyst's Guide to Fiscal Policy,* has authored or coauthored several articles in the *Wall Street Journal* and the *New York Times,* and coauthors the monthly *Economy in Perspective* for A. B. Laffer Associates. He has also done extensive research on the effect of state and local fiscal policies on economic growth, coauthoring studies on fiscal policy in Delaware and Massachusetts, and consulting for the Maryland Growth Coalition Project.

Arthur B. Laffer

Arthur B. Laffer is a Distinguished University Professor at Pepperdine University. Previously, he was the Charles B. Thornton Professor of Business Economics at the University of Southern California and was Associate Professor of Business Economics at the University of Chicago.

Dr. Laffer received a B.A. in Economics from Yale University in 1963, prior to which he also attended the University of Munich, Germany. He received an M.B.A. (1965) and a Ph.D in Economics (1972) from Stanford University.

Dr. Laffer currently is a member of the Economic Policy Advisory Board to the president of the United States. He is also a member of the Policy Committee and Board of Directors of the American Council for Capital Formation (Washington, D.C.). He has received two Graham and Dodd Awards from the Financial Analyst Federation for outstanding feature articles published in the *Financial Analysts Journal.* Dr. Laffer is also founder and Chairman of A. B. Laffer Associates, an economic research and financial consulting firm. He has been a consultant to the Secretaries of Treasury and Defense. He served as the Economist of the Office of Management and Budget from October 1970 through July 1972. Dr. Laffer was also a Research Associate at the Brookings Institution, on leave from the University of Chicago.

Dr. Laffer's other books include *The Financial Analyst's Guide to Fiscal Policy, International Economics in an Integrated World, Future American Energy Policy, The Economics of the Tax Revolt: A Reader, Private Short Term Capital Flows,* and *The Phenomenon of Worldwide Inflation.* His publications have appeared in *American Economic Review, Journal of Political Economy, Journal of Business,* and *Journal of Money Credit and Banking,* among others.